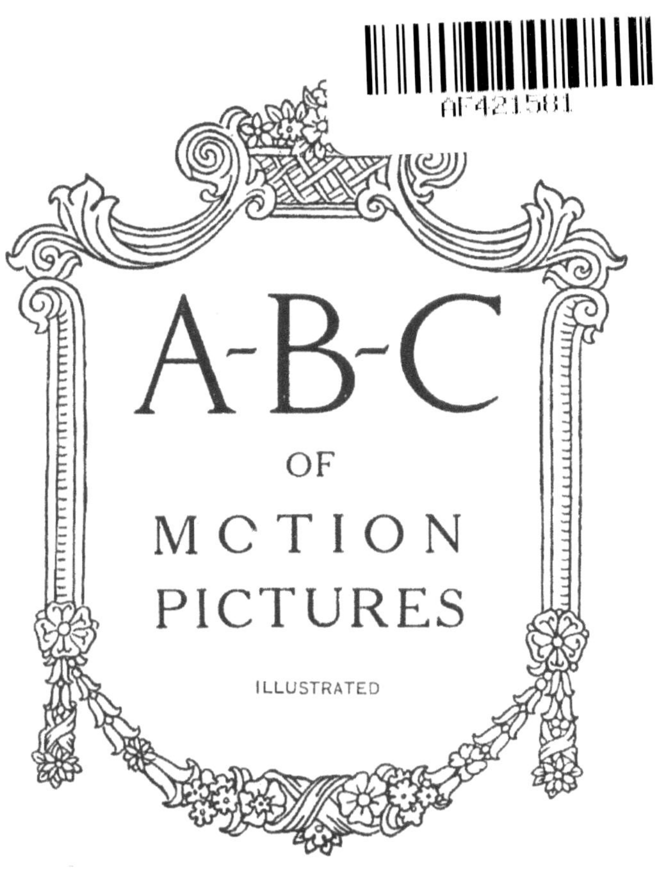

by
Robert E. Welsh

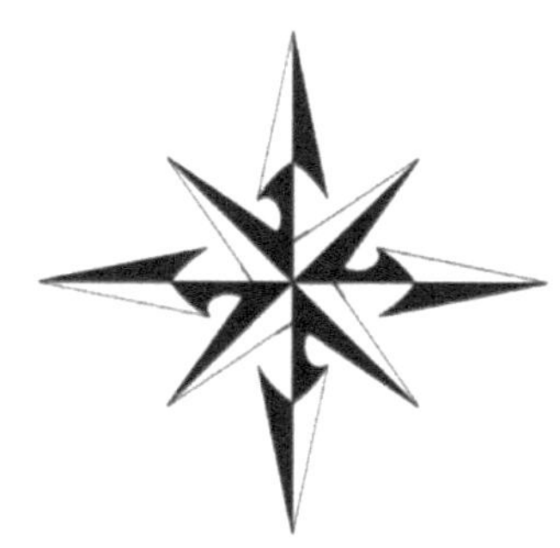

NATAL PUBLISHING LLC

ARS LONGA, VITA BREVIS

FOREWORD

The marvelous development of the motion picture and the important place it has won in the heart of the entire civilized world have attracted an interest never before attained in so short a time by any form of amusement. The author of this volume has commendably explained the essential facts in the history of this popular art, and the principles allied with it of most general interest to the public at large. It contains answers to questions commonly and constantly asked, and I believe that its perusal will be well worth while. ·

Dan'l Frohman.

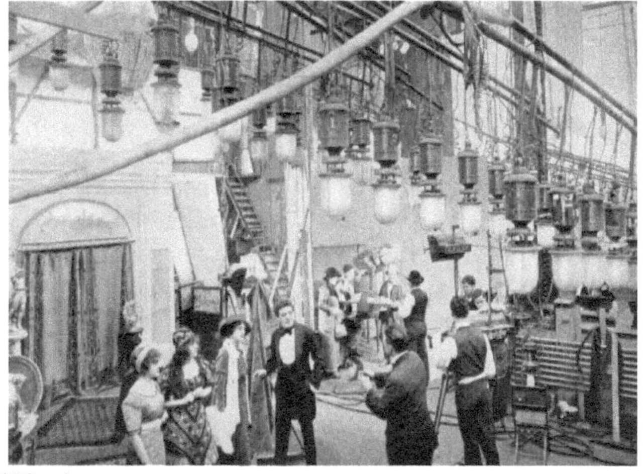

(*Edison*)

Interior of a Typical Motion-Picture Studio

INTRODUCTION

Both as a form of entertainment and as an educational force the motion picture now merits consideration in the front rank of the world's activities. Conservative estimates state that twelve million persons attend the picture theaters of the United States every day. Were figures available for Europe they could not add any to the amazement of those who remember that the motion picture's strides to its present popularity have been taken in a period of less than twenty years.

Perhaps it is because of the rapidity of its growth that the art is still a mystery to the layman. In this book the author has set himself the task of answering the hundred and one questions that must occur frequently to followers of the motion picture. In a logical manner every stage in the process of making motion pictures is covered, while due attention has been paid to the historical and business phases of the subject. A studied effort has been made to use terms clear to the lay mind. With the task completed, it is the conviction of the author that the reader will find his puzzling doubts replaced by a clear understanding that should add immeasurably to his interest in the motion-picture art.

Additional chapters of instruction in the writing of photoplays have been included in the belief that they will meet a widely-felt need for accurate information and authoritative advice on this aspect of the silent drama. Though the book is explanatory throughout, a chapter of specific advice to the amateur organization desirous of staging a motion picture has been provided. This is an untouched field in works on pictures, and one that we believe is steadily becoming of interest to a wider circle.

R. E. W.
New York, *December, 1915.*

I
HISTORY AND PRINCIPLES OF MOTION PICTURES

Like practically all other modern mechanical wonders, the motion picture was not the invention of any one man. Rather, the picture as we know it to-day is the cumulative result of the toil and experiments of a score of workers, whose efforts cover over half a century. As far back as 1795 scientists were striving to produce the phenomena of pictures that moved. Succeeding generations all saw experimenters working toward the same object, each contributing his mite of improvement, until, with Thomas A. Edison's invention of the kinetoscope, in 1893, the day of modern motion pictures dawned.

Though all these seekers for knowledge worked constantly with "pictures of objects in motion" as their goal, it is not possible that any saw in the motion picture the possibility of development to its present important place. Dreamers as they necessarily were, there were no imaginations even among picture-men of the last decade that would dare such wide stretches of fancy. No other artistic or industrial development of history will bear comparison with the motion picture's leap from humble beginnings to exalted favor.

Let us go back to the lowly antecedents of the present-day giant. In the year 1830, we find a description of the zoetrope, or "Wheel of Life," which was introduced in the United States in 1845. Though pretending to be nothing more than a toy, the zoetrope embodied the optical principle that is at the basis of all motion-picture work. It consisted of a revolving cylinder, in appearance much like a common hat-box, with the top removed to permit the light to enter. Vertical slots were made equal spaces apart around the upper half of the cylinder, and ten or more drawings showing a particular object in different positions were placed around the lower half of the interior. The cylinder revolved on a vertical spindle, and the spectator, peering through the slots, received the impression of seeing the object on the interior in motion. Simple drawings were used, a favorite being the figure of a dancer.

The similarity between the zoetrope, despite the fact that it did not make use of photography, and the modern motion picture, lies in the scientific principle responsible for the illusion of moving figures. In viewing a particular object there is the briefest delay in conveying the impression from the eye to the brain, so that the latter has the conception of seeing the object after it has actually passed from the field of vision. If, during this fractional part of a second, another picture of the object, in a slightly different position, is presented to the eye, the brain's sensation will be that of having seen the object move. Were a series of such pictures moved before the eye in rapid succession, the impression registered would seem more like a streak than an object in motion, so that there must be some way of cutting off the vision until the second picture has been moved into the exact position held by the first, and so on. The spaces between the slots in the zoetrope served this purpose, and so rapid was the revolution of the cylinder that the spectator was not aware of having had his vision interrupted, and only received the impression that on a direct line with the eye there was an object which seemed to be moving.

To understand the application of this principle to modern motion pictures let us take a strip of film a foot in length as an example. There are sixteen separate pictures on this piece of film. The screen of the motion-picture theater serves as the fixed point at which the spectator is gazing. One second is required to show this foot of film on the screen, and the spectator is of the opinion that pictures have been shown throughout that entire second. In reality, the shutter of the projection-machine threw each separate picture on the screen for about one thirty-second of a second, and there was an interval of about the same duration while the next picture was being moved into place.

The zoetrope had many successors, as new devices of improvement were discovered. It never became much more than a toy, however, interesting solely because the simple objects shown appeared to move. The next important chapter in motion-picture history concerns the experiments of Edward Muybridge, an Englishman, in 1871-2. Photography had by this time advanced so that it was possible to take pictures with an exposure of less than one-twentieth of a second. Muybridge conceived the plan of using several cameras to photograph an object in motion. Governor Leland Stanford, of California, offered to finance an experiment by which pictures were to be taken of his race-horse, Occident.

Muybridge placed twenty-four cameras along the rail of the California race-track, where the attempt was to be made. Strings were stretched across the track from each of the cameras and adjusted so that when the running horse broke them it would operate the shutter in such a manner that each camera secured a photograph of the animal. Muybridge's success received world-wide notice and set the scientists of Europe and America to renewed efforts to perfect the motion-picture idea. Some progress was made in the decade immediately following, the French worker, Dr. Marey, being especially successful.

But for many reasons Muybridge's methods, and those of his followers, were not fitted to practical use. These faults all found their basis in the necessity of using cumbersome glass plates in making the photographs, so the search began for a flexible substance on which pictures could be taken. Gelatine was utilized in many different ways, with little success; preparations of all sorts were tried on paper. Our own Edison was working on the problem in the early eighties, and made many important discoveries regarding pictures, but they were not to see practical application until the invention of celluloid film.

History, in this case found in dusty court records, awards the priority of patent on the process of making motion-picture film to the Rev. Hannibal Goodwin, of Newark, New Jersey. In the years between 1885 and 1887 the clergyman, working independently, and George Eastman, experimenting with his co-worker, Walker, evolved a flexible film of which celluloid was the basis. Eastman's company began the manufacture of the film on a large scale, and waxed strong, while Goodwin, and later his heirs, were forced to a court battle that did not end until 1914, when a final decision was given in favor of the owners of the Goodwin patents. At present the Eastman Company manufactures practically all of the world's film supply under an arrangement with the holders of the Newark clergyman's patents.

When Edison saw that the flexible film was successful in ordinary photography he again turned to serious work on motion pictures, and the Chicago World's Fair, held in 1893, saw the introduction of his kinetoscope. This was a coin-in-the-slot device and a nickel was the charge at that time to view a picture about thirty seconds in duration. The novelty soon wore off, mainly because the pictures were so short, and Edison placed the kinetoscope on the shelf. Apparently foreign mechanical workers attending the Fair thought more of the apparatus than did its inventor, for in the years immediately following they made many advances on the original model, while Edison had even neglected to patent his invention abroad. Paul in London, Lumière in France, and numerous others were at work, and by 1896 signs of their success were apparent. The result was that Edison again turned to his kinetoscope, and soon he presented an improved machine, the vitascope, which could be used in theaters to show pictures on a screen.

The motion picture was here. It was not long before pictures were being shown in theaters in Paris and London, and in July, 1896, Lumière's cinematograph was exhibited at the Union Square Theater in New York. Others entered the field, some of the pioneers being Siegmund Lubin, William N. Selig, Henry Marvin, George Kleine, Francis Marion, William T. Rock, Albert E. Smith, and J. Stuart Blackton. These early picture-men were also, by necessity, somewhat capable as inventors, and numerous patents were secured on different portions of the apparatus for making and exhibiting pictures. The next few years of the industry's history is the tale of numerous patent suits that wound in and out of the courts. The legal battles accentuated the naturally bitter competition to be expected in exploiting the new wonder. But the public had given a hearty welcome to the latest form of entertainment, and the picture-makers waxed prosperous, despite the handicap of internal strife. Theaters in all the big cities were showing the pictures as novelties, and traveling exhibitors were frequent. The "store show," a picture theater made by remodeling a common store, came into being, and to supply them with pictures exchanges were opened all over the country. These exchanges were the "middle-men" of the picture field, buying the films from the manufacturers, and in turn renting them to the theater-owners.

The patent litigation came to an end in 1908 when a group of the most important companies united to protect their patents, and to distribute their output through a common channel. For a time it seemed that the motion picture was to become a monopoly. But the independents, by co-operation with foreign manufacturers, succeeded in maintaining their position, so that the field is to-day as open to individual activity as any other line of commercial effort.

In the years immediately preceding the organization of this group of the biggest concerns, the picture itself was not progressing. There was no longer any novelty in seeing people in motion on the screen, and the inane subjects shown offered little more than that. While the pessimists, who, as a matter of fact, had never taken a deep interest in the motion picture, were predicting its early demise, the manufacturers set about to find means of renewing the interest. Short dramas and comedies were written, and players drafted from the stage. The public responded readily, and once more Fortune smiled upon the picture-men, never again to desert them.

Until about 1911 the average motion picture was approximately one thousand feet long, and occasionally two or more distinct subjects were included on a piece of film this length. The reels on which the film is wound for easy handling will hold one thousand feet, so that in the United States a picture of this length came to be known as a "single-reel" picture. In England and on the Continent this term has not come into general use, the practice being to state the approximate length of the film in feet or meters. Though Richard G. Holloman's three-thousand-foot or three-reel production of "The Passion Play," in 1905, had proved most profitable, the American manufacturers did not heed the indication that audiences would welcome stories longer than one thousand feet. Foreign producers were quicker to see the possibilities of the longer picture, but as recently as 1912 their productions of greater length than two thousand feet were offered without response on the American market. Then came the success of "Quo Vadis?" an Italian multiple-reel picture, exploited in this country by George Kleine, of Chicago, to whom credit must be given for the rise of the long production, with its results in placing the picture in the best theaters in the country. "Quo Vadis?" earned a fortune, and was followed by a scramble on the part of buyers to get the long-neglected foreign productions, while the American manufacturers turned their attention to the staging of multiple-reel pictures.

To-day the short picture, though still forming the bulk of the output, is somewhat neglected, for the quickest way to the public's fancy seems to lie in the big production that rivals the stage-play. In Europe the long picture is declining in favor, and the picture of one and two thousand feet returning to popularity. In the United States, however, it would seem that the future of the motion picture lies in the production that gives an entire evening's entertainment, offering, as it does, opportunities for the exercise of artistic effort that are denied by the fifteen or thirty minute picture.

II
THE STUDIO—THE MECHANICS OF PICTURE MAKING AND SHOWING

Picture studios dot the map of the world. One or more will be found in practically every capital of Europe. In France there are three principal manufacturing companies, each with a chain of studios. Germany and the Scandinavian countries likewise produce a number of pictures, while Italy ranks second to France in the European field. For reasons probably finding their root in the stolid British temperament, England has not kept pace with France, Italy, and the United States as a producer of film. Within recent years, however, there have been signs of an awakening on the part of the English which should give to that country a more fitting place in the new art.

Los Angeles and New York, and the territory around these cities, share the honors as picture-producing centers in the United States. Several other large cities have picture studios, however, and the list is constantly being added to by the search for new settings or the enterprise of local capitalists. New York has been found to be ideal as a location because of the variety of scenery, from seashore to crowded city street or pretty rural settings within easy reach. But southern California, with almost continuous sunshine, has become the picture Mecca and it is estimated that over one-half of the world's picture-supply is made there.

Around New York the studios are almost all solely for indoor work, the producers using the "highways and byways" for their outdoor scenes. In California, however, several of the companies own estates covering many hundreds of acres, and it is seldom necessary to go off the company's property to take any scene desired. Dotting the estates you will find village streets that would seem to have been transplanted from the four corners of the globe. Well-stocked zoos, that would be the prize possession of many a municipality, are a unique feature of some of these plants. Philadelphia also boasts of a large picture-producing estate of this type. Indoor studios may be recognized by the glass top and sides, an evidence of the desire for sunlight. Mercury lights and electric arc-lights are the means of illumination used for work at night or on days when the sun's rays do not prove sufficient.

A knowledge of the workings of the motion-picture camera is essential to a clear understanding of the chapters that follow, so it might be well to include that here. You have seen the large box camera employed in the ordinary photographer's gallery. The motion-picture camera appears very much like an enlarged box camera, with the addition of a crank on the side and a dial to measure the amount of film used. It is mounted on a tripod which is also movable, either laterally or horizontally, by means of cranks. In all essential points motion-picture photography is really continuous snap-shot photography. Celluloid film is used, that for motion-picture purposes being one and three-eighth inches wide, and supplied in long strips, the average length being two hundred feet. By turning the crank at the side the motion photographer is able to get continuous photographs of a person or object in motion, instead of the single picture that the snap-shot photographer gets. As each of these photographs is only three-quarters of an inch high, it will be seen that the cinematographer can take sixteen separate photographs on each foot of film in his camera. This "sixteen" is a cabalistic figure in motion pictures. There are sixteen photographs on each foot of film. For average work the camera-man photographs the pictures at the rate of sixteen to the second, and they are shown on the screen in the picture theater at the same speed.

When the camera-man turns the crank at the side of his camera two independent mechanisms are affected by the operation, the shutter and the device for feeding the film. The shutter is opened to allow the brief exposure of the film necessary to take a single picture, and it is then closed while another three-quarter inch of film is moved into position ready for the next picture. The camera-man continues to turn his crank, thus repeating the operation over and over again until the entire scene is photographed.

The shutter in motion-picture cameras is a revolving disk, in which a "V"-shaped opening is cut, or also the aperture may be formed by two disks superimposed, in which case the operator is able to vary the size of the opening. The operator's crank is connected by gears to the shutter, which is placed between the lens and the film. The action of the shutter has been explained in the paragraph above. It might be stated here that the exposure of the film is a trifle longer than that which would be allowed by the ordinary snap-shot photographer, since the blurring which results on the picture is indistinguishable, owing to the rapidity with which the photographs follow each other on the screen.

Two light-tight boxes are contained in the camera, one at the top to hold the raw film, and the lower one to receive the film after it has been exposed. Perforations have been made along the edges of the film before it is placed in the camera, the holes being oblong in shape, one-eighth of an inch wide and one-sixteenth of an inch in height. The film-feeding device, which is either of the sprocket-wheel type, which drives the film through, or the claw-hammer type, which pulls it, engages in these holes. The perforations serve a similar purpose in the camera, the projection-machine, and in the process of developing the negative and printing the positives. It will be seen that the perforating, which is done by machinery, must be accurate to the one-hundredth of an inch.

The working of the projection-machine, the apparatus which throws the image on the film onto the screen, is in many ways similar to that of the camera. Or, a simpler comparison, the projection-machine is really the familiar stereopticon, or magic lantern, with the addition of mechanism for feeding the film rapidly before the light and the lenses. In the first place, there is a "lamp-house," a small cabinet which contains the light, supplied by means of an arc-light, and the condensing lens. The light created by the carbons of the arc, while strong, is diffused in the lamp-house, and it is the purpose of the condensing lenses to concentrate the rays before throwing them on the screen. The pictures are outlined on the screen because of the fact that the figures on the film obstruct light in proportion to their density.

From the lamp-house and the condensing lenses we naturally pass to consideration of the film, and the devices by which it is fed before the rays of light with such accuracy that the picture is always in place on the screen, and with such rapidity and uniformity of speed that the spectator is not aware of the fact that he is really looking at sixteen separate pictures each second. The principle of the operation is similar to that used in the camera. The film passes from a fire-proof magazine above, being pulled out by a sprocket-wheel that engages in the perforations. After passing from these sprockets there is a brief respite for the film, a loop being provided to relieve it so that the pull will not be too great when passing through the film-gate which holds the image in place before the rays of the condenser. It is necessary that the gate hold the film perfectly taut and in alignment, for it can be seen that the slightest fractional deviation would appear great when the image is magnified by the objective lenses onto the screen.

Below the film-gate we find another sprocket-wheel, this one to pull the film through the gate, being operated by an intermittent movement. This movement brings the required length of film before the condensing lens's rays, allows it to remain there the necessary length of time, and then repeats the operation over and over until the entire reel is shown.

Improvements in projection-machines, and especially in the "intermittent movement," have eliminated the flickering, "jumpy" pictures we remember so well only a few years ago. The film is put in motion by a crank at the side of the machine, operated either by hand or by electric power. It is the function of the intermittent movement to convert this rotary motion into the short rectilinear motions that move the film, with the corresponding rests while it is being shown. The principal type of intermittent movement consists of a revolving "pin"wheel, operated by the turning of the crank. The pin engages in the arm of another wheel, a cross in shape, which makes one-quarter of a revolution, and, since it is connected to the sprocket-wheel, thus pulls the film through the gate. At the completion of its down stroke the pinwheel necessarily disengages with the arm of the cross and continues to revolve. But the cross is idle, so the film is held firm in the gate until the pinwheel completes the circle and engages with the next arm of the cross. This will serve the purpose of explaining the principle of the intermittent movement, though improvements and variations are constantly being made.

The portions of the projection-machine yet unexplained are the objective lens and the shutter. The lens, which is immediately in front of the film-gate, receives the rays of light passing through the film from the condenser and throws them on the screen. The shutter, which is usually of the revolving-disk type, interrupts the light while the film is being moved to allow the next photograph to reach the correct position. It may be remarked here that the film cannot be allowed to remain in the film-gate indefinitely, for the intense heat of the light from the condenser would soon ignite it. This occasionally happens when the film buckles, and the operator's first thought when there is trouble with his machine is to shut off the light. Safety fire appliances prevent the blaze from spreading beyond the film-gate.

The motion photographer is able with the aid of his camera to perform any number of miraculous feats. He can have one man play two or three parts on the screen at one time, thus having an actor engage in conversation with himself, and so on. And then, readers are most likely all familiar with the pictures showing magical appearances and disappearances of characters. Or the picture-maker can give you a thrilling view of the burning of a city, yet he need not have journeyed outside the studio or expended more than a few dollars to get the scene.

The use of models built in exact miniature explains the producer's ability to burn a thriving metropolis to the ground so easily. The wreck of an ocean liner is another feat accomplished in a small tank with papier-maché models. When photographed with the camera comparatively close these scenes appear on the screen to be absolutely realistic, though to the spectator in the theater it seems that the camera was placed at a great distance. Readers who remember the startling volcanic eruption shown in "Cabiria" have evidence of the remarkable deceiving power of the models.

Plays with twin brothers or sisters in the principal rôles became popular with picture producers after they discovered that it was possible to have one player appear simultaneously in the two parts. This is accomplished by "double exposure," which, as the words indicate, is performed by exposing the same strip of film twice. Take the case mentioned, the showing of twin brothers, as an example. First a hair-line division is made of the stage, marking off the two parts on which the different brothers are to appear. Then the scene on one side of the stage is photographed, the film on the other side being protected from exposure—"masked" is the technical term. Following the photographing of this scene, the actor playing the twin brothers steps to the other side of the stage and, with the action already photographed now "masked," the same strip of film is run through the camera. When the picture is developed it will appear as though two actors appeared in the scene. In making such scenes the director of the production makes use of a split-second watch in order that the action may be timed perfectly and that on both sides of the film chime correctly. It can be seen that a slip of a fraction of a second can easily make the character's actions appear ridiculous. Despite the difficulties of the work, however, it has become quite common, and daring directors have gone so far as to have dual characters, played by one person, clasp each other's hands. Where physical contact is attempted, it will be seen that the director, in addition to accurately timing the action on both sides of the film, must have a marker that will note to the fraction of an inch the point at which the character stretched his hand outside the camera's range, so that, when the other side of the film is photographed, the joining will be perfect. A thread, invisible to the camera, and stretched from above the stage to the floor will serve this purpose.

A type of double-exposure work that is, perhaps, even more familiar to readers is that used in showing visions, as, for instance, when the producer desires to show the thoughts that are passing through a character's mind. The vision may appear in one of the upper corners of the scene, the more common method, or, for novelty's sake, it may form on the pages of a book the character is reading. The principle in these cases is similar to that explained in the twin-brothers scene. First the action covering most of the scene is photographed, with that part of the film masked on which the vision is to appear. Then the same strip of film is run through the camera to photograph the players enacting the action of the vision. It will be readily apparent that in this work the camera's perspective must be altered, where in the twin-brother scene it was necessary that there be no change in the position of the camera until both scenes were photographed.

The magical appearances and disappearances of characters will be simple to readers who now understand the operation of the motion-picture camera. They will see that it is an easy matter to have a character disappear by ceasing to turn the crank, covering the lens, and then having the character walk off the scene, after which the turning of the crank is resumed. When the picture is developed the player will be seen up to a certain point, then he will suddenly disappear, but the other objects in the scene will appear unchanged. In the same manner a person can be brought suddenly on the scene, appearing to spring from the air. Trick effects may also be secured by running the film through the camera backward, and reversing the actions of the players, that is, making them "do things backward." When the film is run through the projection-machine correctly, and shown on the screen, you see the player perform such miraculous feats as jumping from the middle of a river clear up a steep bank, when in reality to take the picture he leaped backward from the bank to the river—but the film was reversed.

In securing all these effects the producer does not fail to make use of the power of suggestion in the mind of the audience. For instance, the amazing disappearance will be accompanied by the ignition of a smoke-pot, so that it will appear that the character "went up in smoke," a decidedly more impressive effect than to have him of a sudden vanish into thin air. The latter appears too artificial. In photographing visions, also, the camera's eye will be narrowed, then gradually widened, so that the audience imagines it can see the figures taking shape and form. With the use of models especially the power of suggestion must be adroitly employed, for, if given undistracted opportunity to examine a scene, the audience would quickly note its artificiality. If a producer were forced to use models in depicting a train wreck, for example, he would be careful to work up to it by showing views of real trains speeding along the rails, and even actual views of the spot at which the wreck was to occur. The models would then be built in exact duplicate of this spot. Flashes of the model trains rushing to destruction would then be interspersed with close-up views of the characters in the story, who, we will say, are supposed to be on one of the trains, or else they are rushing to a switch in a vain attempt to prevent the wreck. Following the crash of the trains the producer would be quick to give us close-up views of a real train wreck, probably taken months before by a news photographer, or else he might batter a studio-built car, upset a smoke-pot or two, and have the characters in the story rush about in the dimly lit—but apparently harrowing—scene. The different scenes might be taken days, weeks, or even months apart, yet when joined together by a careful producer the effect would be that of a swift, onrushing climax.

What about talking-pictures and natural-color films? is one of the first questions asked by the layman. He remembers that perfect talking-pictures were announced some years ago, and that kinemacolor pictures which reproduce all the coloring of nature have long been on the market. Why have they not crowded the old black-and-white and silent pictures out? Let us take the talking-picture first. The illusion of seeing the characters and hearing them speak at the same time is produced by the synchronization of a phonograph and the picture-projector. Now, while perfect timing can be secured, no way has been found to keep the synchronization perfect. A scratch on the talking-machine record, for example, can be seen to result disastrously if it jumps the conversation a word in advance of the figure on the screen. Again, motion-picture film must undergo considerable wear in the projection-machine and frequently the perforations are torn. The operator will then cut the torn piece out and paste the film together once more. The lost bit of action is not noticed on the screen; the pictures follow one another too rapidly for that. But a corresponding change cannot be made in the talking-record, and it does not require many patches to throw film and phonograph out of time. It is possible that these mechanical difficulties will be overcome, and also that the talking-picture will be perfected so that, instead of the simplest of scenes as at present, it will be able to depict the entire action of an ambitious drama, but to-day it is clear that the picture patron greatly prefers the silent drama.

Natural-color films, which are taken by means of two cameras, photographing separately the red and green rays of the spectrum, the two being superimposed in projection, though more successful than the talking-pictures, have failed of being universally adopted. The brilliance of the pictures was found to be tiring to the eyes, while the depiction of rapid action without the presence of a blur or "fringe" around the characters was found difficult. Open-air stages and ideal conditions were necessary to secure the full benefit of the sun, and the requirement for a specially designed projection-machine proved a handicap. But the prophet would be foolish who would pronounce either natural-color or talking-pictures as dead because of early failures.

III
MOTION-PICTURE SUBJECTS

The camera's eye may roam the world for subjects; its range equals that of the newspaper or magazine. The stage and literature, travel, science, news and advertising, all are open to the motion picture. The photoplay, presenting a visualized story, is the most popular form, for the public heeds quickest the call of entertainment. But serious students of the motion picture believe that, in time, its purely amusement features will be dwarfed by the development along lines that may be roughly grouped under the heading "educational."

Even to-day the news pictorial is one of the most interesting and profitable of motion-picture subjects. Five of the picture companies have representatives stationed all over the globe, gathering material for these "animated newspapers," while there are scores of small companies covering limited territories with a direct appeal to local picture theaters. The news pictorial camera-man must be as alert as his stepbrother, the reporter, for the competition is every bit as keen as that in the newspaper field, and a victory over a rival just as great cause for elation. But the photographer must be "on the spot" while his news is happening, so that his work is much more difficult and his field limited. Furthermore, the camera-man's news must, either by its importance or its human interest, have an appeal to the entire country, and the ideal piece of "news-film" is that which may also be used abroad. Especially disastrous fires, which can often be photographed while they are happening, the effects of train wrecks or other accidents, personages prominent in the news of the day, all these are grist for the camera-man's mill. Parades are the bane of the pictorial editor's life, for he knows that lengthy views are not of great interest, yet he is often forced to use them because of the scarcity of views of real news events. Occasionally the editor of the news pictorial will create his own news by having a daredevil perform some unusual feat.

When the representative has taken his picture the negative is rushed to the headquarters, where it is developed, and the editor starts to work assembling the film that has been received from the different field men. Often there are little office tragedies when the film is developed and it is found that a singularly interesting piece of film must be thrown away because of poor photography. The news camera-man cannot make his own conditions; he must take big chances, for the news will not wait for him. After the editor has assembled the film that he can use, subtitles are written, and the completed films shipped to the various exchanges, which distribute them to the theaters. The greatest handicaps the news pictorial has had to overcome are the difficulty of getting the film to the theaters while the news is fresh, and the fact that the news picture's life is short. A dramatic picture will live, that is, earn money by rentals to exhibitors, almost indefinitely, but the news-film that is two months old is practically ready for the shelf.

Commercial reasons have likewise retarded the development of the educational picture. Indeed, in view of the return that it was possible, until recently, to secure from educational pictures, one must compliment the manufacturers on the moderate attention they have bestowed on the subject. Theater-managers have always been wary of offering their audiences pictures that were avowedly educational, so that the income from this source has always been small. Within the past few years, however, schools and other institutions of an educational character have devoted more attention to the possibilities of the motion picture, and the development of systematic and profitable methods of distribution is likely. Once this is brought about, the growth in importance of the educational picture is certain to be astounding.

The "industrial," which is the trade term for the picture that is used to advertise a particular product, is another field that has been only slightly touched. There are a number of companies that specialize in such work, but the stumbling-block thus far has been the exhibitor's unwillingness to show the pictures in his theater. He rightly feels that the patron who has paid to see the performance feels cheated when his time is taken up with a strictly advertising picture. Many of these "industrials" can be made very interesting, however, by weaving light stories around the product to be advertised, so that the advertiser achieves his purpose indirectly and without the necessity of throwing his sermon broadside at the spectator.

We recollect one such subject which was circulated by the makers of a brand of ready-made women's clothes. An elaborate social function was the basis of the story, and two women who had been invited to the affair the principal characters. One patronized a select Fifth Avenue tailor who disappointed her at the eleventh hour and forced madam to wear an old gown to the function. This tragedy to the female heart was avoided by the second woman. More resourceful than her sister, she purchased the advertised brand of apparel at a department store and was later the envied center of attraction at the society affair. To drive home his lesson the author now had the patron of exclusive modistes visit a relative who lived in the city that was the home of the ready-to-wear clothes. An invitation to visit the factory followed, and the camera carried us along with madam through all the interesting departments. Though it was advertising, such a picture could not fail to appeal to women.

Many artists have entered the picture field either by means of the animated cartoon, in which the figures seem endowed with life, or the picture that shows the artist drawing his sketches. Since sixteen separate drawings must be made for each foot of film it will readily be seen that the work is long and laborious. The strong lights necessary for photographing the pictures also make it trying for the artist, who must work directly beneath the camera. Mechanical contrivances are called upon to lessen the artist's troubles as much as possible, and many ingenious schemes are resorted to in order to photograph rapidly a series of pictures. For instance, the artist may draw the head, arms, body, and limbs of a figure and then, by means of tabs, move them about under glass plates so as to secure the impression of animation. The idea of perspective may be secured by drawing the object in different sizes, to the proper scale, of course, and then bringing the object forward from a distance by using gradually increasing figures, or, by reversing the process, carrying the object away. "Stop" cameras are used, which remain idle while the artist is moving his figures for the next photograph. Even with all the recent inventions to facilitate the work, animated cartoons are by no means easily made, and a film that can be shown on the screen in ten minutes is a good week's labor for the artist.

And now we come to the photoplay—the picture that tells a story by means of actors. "Where do the stories come from?" is one of the first questions asked by the layman, though the adapted plays and novels provide their own answer. But what of the ordinary picture stories that form the bulk of the offerings on the screen? Are they bought, like magazine stories, from writers who submit to all the magazines, or are they turned out by staff writers who provide all the stories needed by each company? How much do the companies pay for the stories? How can I enter this profession? The questions are innumerable. Let us answer them in turn.

The first motion-picture stories, following on the period of trick pictures and other simple scenes, when there was still some novelty in seeing pictures that moved, were concocted by the directors and players from day to day, and were usually of a very simple nature. But the producers were showmen enough to see that the public wanted even better stories, and each studio soon had its staff writer or two, usually former newspaper-men, who wrote all the stories required by the players. But the motion picture soon outgrew this period, the staffs of writers at the studios increased in size, and the call for stories from outside writers was heard. During the past few years an increasing number of the stories have been from the pens of outside writers, who send their wares to all the studios just as the ordinary author submits his manuscripts to the different publishers. The latest phase is the demand for the highest quality of stories by the purchase of play and novel rights for long pictures, and magazine short-story rights for the short films.

The staff writer continues, for the producing companies cannot rely on the outside writer, though thousands of stories are submitted each week. And even the stories accepted must usually be rewritten by the staff writer to suit the requirements of his company.

For many reasons the profession of photoplay-writing is not as rosy as one would be led to believe by some of the advertisements of correspondence schools. The prices paid for stories are not very high, though it can be said that they are steadily increasing, and the author of really good work has little difficulty in securing very good rates. From fifteen to fifty dollars may be paid for one-reel stories—that is, pictures that require about fifteen minutes to show. Longer stories are usually paid for at the same basis per reel, though here again the well-known author may demand his own price, or an exceptionally good idea bring a special reward.

Another fact that renders the writing of picture stories more profitable for the beginner as an avocation than a vocation, is the necessity of meeting unusually trying conditions. Like the magazines, the companies favor particular types, but a more binding rule is the necessity of securing stories that suit the requirements of the particular company's players, or the locality in which the pictures are being staged at the time. There are a multitude of smaller circumstances that may weigh for or against the purchase of stories regardless of the question of merit. The staff writer knows these conditions, his stories are written while the iron is hot, and he is always ready when called upon.

Say to any photoplay editor or manufacturer, "Are you buying stories from the outside now?" and his reply is certain—it seldom changes. "We are—if we can get them," he tells you. This does not mean that he is not receiving stories; there is scarcely a studio whose mail is not overloaded with manuscripts. Nor does it mean that the stories he accepts must be worthy of being placed on the screen at once as they are written, for the scenario editor takes it for granted that the scripts purchased will have to be rewritten. It is because over ninety per cent. of the stories received are absolutely impossible; one editor places the figure at ninety-eight per cent. In later chapters we will take up more fully the reasons which place these manuscripts in the "rejected" class.

It was their inability to secure a steady supply of good stories from the picture ranks that drove the producers to the magazine field. The entry of the well-known stage-player into pictures and the growth in popularity of the long photoplay caused the purchase of novels and plays. In addition to the large sums paid outright for these subjects the owner of the original rights usually receives a royalty on the earnings of the picture. Staff-men employed by the picture companies adapt the plays and novels to the form suitable for presentation by means of motion pictures.

The censoring of pictures is a subject of interest to those who aspire to write photoplays. In choosing his theme the amateur must remember that the manufacturer is not anxious to invest money in the production of a subject that will later have to lie idle on the shelf because it will not pass the censors. The most important censoring body, the National Board of Censorship, was established voluntarily by the manufacturers in co-operation with the People's Institute of New York. The members of the board, who are appointed from various sociological organizations, serve without remuneration, the only paid employees being the secretaries. The expenses of the organization are borne by the manufacturers. The National Board has been of considerable benefit to the motion-picture industry, a fact largely due to the whole-hearted support of the manufacturers. A manufacturer cannot, of course, be compelled to submit his pictures for the approval of the board, but at present more than ninety-five per. cent. of the pictures shown in this country are viewed by its score or more of voluntary committees. The censors see the pictures at the New York offices of the producers, usually far enough in advance to permit of making any changes they may order before the pictures are distributed. In addition, state and municipal bodies have been established in many sections of the country. If you intend taking up photoplay work seriously, write the National Board of Censorship, 70 Fifth Avenue, New York City, for a pamphlet explaining its principles of judgment. It will be worth your while.

IV
STAGING A PICTURE

The cost of producing a motion picture which provides a full evening's entertainment averages between ten thousand and twenty-five thousand dollars. One-reel pictures, which require about fifteen minutes to show in a theater, usually cost in the neighborhood of a thousand dollars to produce. It may easily be said that this money is spent by one man—the motion-picture director—yet, with all his responsibility, the director is a character little known to the layman.

Within the picture ranks the terms "director" and "producer" have become interchangeable, though not always correctly so. Directors of the best type are deserving of the title "producer," because their completed productions bear evidence in every branch of their imagination and creative ability. But the more common type of director is really little more than a "stage-manager"; he takes the story as it comes from the author's hands and, "following instructions," stages the manuscript for the camera. He tells the players what they are to do in each scene, lays out the scenic requirements, and so on, but injects none of his own individuality into the pictures. Between the two extremes there is the average director, and it is of his work that we shall treat here.

Who, then, is the motion-picture director? We have explained in a preceding chapter that he is "the man in charge of the making of the picture." But here we shall see him at close range, from the time he receives the story from the photoplay editor until he finally turns his negative film into the factory for developing and editing, after which the positive prints are made. Between the manuscript and the completed film many an interesting event has happened. Perhaps a factory has been burned to the ground, and the heroine rescued from almost certain death; mayhap a daring criminal has run amuck, only to be brought to bay by the noted detective and captured after a thrilling fight; or it is possible that armies have clashed in battle before a battery of cameras. But one and all—heroine, criminal, detective, and soldier—have answered to the beck and call of a director. "The world's a stage," and the picture producer's world is limited only by the imagination of the author.

With his story in hand a director's first task is to select the players for the different characters in the plot. Each studio has a large staff of "stock" players—that is, actors and actresses who are engaged permanently and who may appear in as many as fifty different rôles within a year. The most important of these players are grouped into smaller companies, placed under the charge of a particular director. Each of these players is suited to a particular type of characterization, and the director now assigns the principal parts in his story to the players for whom they are suited. For the minor rôles he will draw on the stock players not assigned to any particular company. If the story has scenes calling for the use of hundreds of characters, such as a ball-room scene, the Stock Exchange, or a battle, he will call for "extras," who are engaged by the day, either from the numerous applicants always to be found waiting expectantly around the studios, or through agents who make a business solely of supplying these supernumeraries to the picture producers.

In the case of long pictures, or "features," as the trade term is, a prominent stage-player is often engaged for the leading rôle. In the selection of his supporting company the director will now be forced to consider the type and characteristics of the "star," and if the latter be gifted with "temperament," the days following are likely to be anything but pleasant. One of the classics of studio history tells of a famous actress, probably one of the best known in America, who was engaged to appear in a picture to be made abroad to secure the correct atmosphere. The company planned to produce the picture in six weeks, but the leading woman's uncontrollable disposition held up the work until six months were actually expended on the undertaking. Petty fits of temper caused this actress to refuse to appear before the camera for days in succession, while at other times she would abandon the work in the middle of a scene, and scarce a move was made that was not preceded by a wordy argument with the director. But, while comparatively common a few years ago, such occurrences are now very rare, with the dividing line between players of the screen and stage not so sharply drawn.

Several preliminary details still await the director. A "scene plot" must be laid out, to let the studio carpenter know what settings will be required by the story, and a list of furnishings and small articles necessary is prepared for the "property-man." Most directors will now read the complete story to the principal players, both that they may understand the action and to allow them to make preparations for the different costumes they will need. A decision will also be made at this time on the particular places that will be used for the exterior scenes. The directors study closely the country around their studios, and some even make use of card indexes to catalogue the spots that may be used at some future time as backgrounds for picture scenes. A house of quaint Colonial architecture, a picturesque brook, or a winding road shaded with stately trees, all will find their place in the director's list, for who knows what scenery his next story may call for?

I know you are impatient to have the camera set up, and to see the action of the photoplay begin. But one more preliminary decision remains for the director before he can do this. He must prepare his "working script," which will outline the order in which he is to produce the different scenes of the story. It is a surprise to most laymen to learn that the scenes in a motion picture are not taken consecutively as they appear on the screen. This would appear to be the more logical and artistic method, but a little investigation will show that this is not practicable. Take, for instance, a story in which a hotel lobby scene appears many times. Were the picture taken in the order in which it is seen when completed the expense on this scene would be repeated several times, since it would be necessary to rebuild the hotel lobby each time the director came to that particular scene in his story, or else use up valuable studio floor space for an idle set while waiting for the director to reach the point where the scene was required again. On the other hand, under the method actually followed, when the hotel lobby is constructed the players can, with little loss of time, go through the different bits of action taking place in this setting. Later, when the film is developed, these scenes will be arranged in their proper place in the story.

Many considerations will be weighed by the director in making up his mind as to the order in which he will take his scenes. The weather, of course, is an important factor in coming to a decision as to whether he will first take his "interiors," that is, scenes taken in the studio, or the "exteriors," the action photographed outdoors. Usually the more simple scenes will be taken first, and the elaborate and costly ones last, this to forestall prohibitive expense should minor changes be made in the story while the picture is being produced. Such changes are not infrequent, for a director will often see ways to strengthen his story while the players are enacting it before his eyes.

We are ready to start to work. It is nine A.M., or perhaps even earlier, for the picture producer does not care to lose any more of the precious daylight than he has to. This is one of the biggest surprises of screen work to the player from the stage. He is accustomed to matinée performances at two in the afternoon, twice a week, but as a usual thing his work is from eight to eleven in the evening. His life is run after the sun has set. Then he enters the picture field and finds it an "early to bed and early to rise" game. Healthful days in the open of green fields and country roads replace the stuffy stage, and even the studio is freedom when compared with the theater. It is the zest and regularity of picture life; yes, even the necessity of awakening early in the morning, that causes so many players from the stage to take it up permanently. There is the real home life of the ordinary professional man, instead of the weary traveling and "one-night stands," and there is employment fifty-two weeks in the year in place of the short season and long lay-off of the theater.

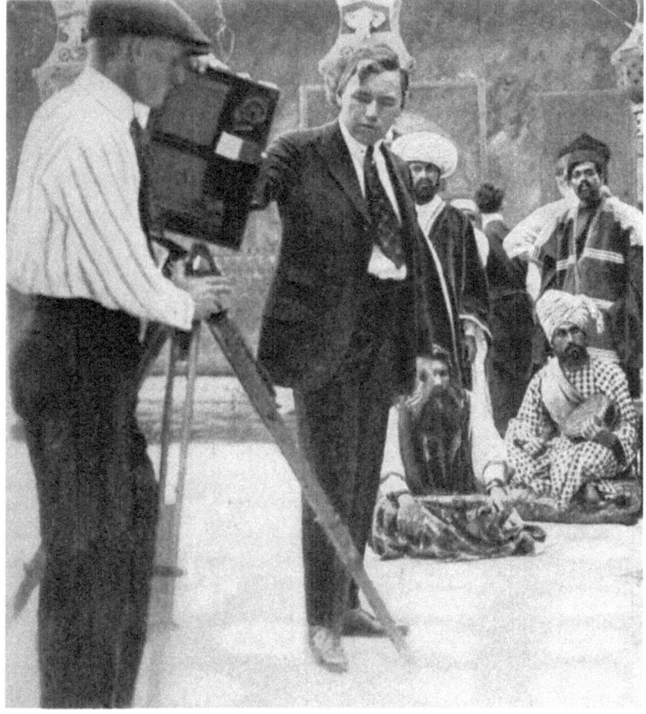

(*Keystone*)

The Director—His Camera and Camera-Man

The sun is shining clearly and the director plans a long day of work in the open. Besides, the studio stages are all in use by directors who have put in their requisitions far in advance. The camera-man and his apparatus, players, and director jump into autos and speed to the first "location." With his assistant the director has mapped the locations and the order of photographing the scenes there as already explained. His first location is a suburban home, one that may be labeled in his catalogue as "home of a fairly wealthy family." A caretaker is in charge and the director knows—from experience—that a few cigars, or, if the house is especially necessary, a greenback, will enable him to use it for picture-taking purposes. We will say that the scenes are to show a thief entering the house and later leaving it with his booty. In the story this is probably to happen at night, but tinting the film blue will later attend to that.

Perhaps there is a tall fence around the grounds, and one of the director's scenes will have to show the thief climbing this obstacle, both on his entry into the grounds, and later on his escape. Perhaps, with the latter, there is to be a brief scuffle with the watchman. A spot for the scene is chosen, the camera set up, and all is ready. The range of vision of the camera's eye, the lens, is an angle, and care is taken to indicate to the players the boundaries of that angle. Outside those lines the players may group themselves idly, but within the lines the camera registers everything, once the crank is turning. The first scene taken is to show the thief scaling the fence. The player is rehearsed once or twice, perhaps even oftener, until he does the action in the exact way the director wishes it done. When he is proficient the director stations himself beside the camera-man, the scene is cleared, and the thief stands waiting just outside the line. "One—two—three—Go!" shouts the director, and at his last word the thief skulks on the scene, the camera-man starts to turn the crank. The thief peers through the fence, glances furtively about him, and then, as if making a sudden decision, starts to climb. He drops to the ground on the other side, then runs diagonally until he is again outside the camera line. It is over. During the whole the director has been the busiest man on the spot. Each motion of the player has been accompanied by a command from him, but it is not for the player to let the camera know that he is listening for these words. By holding a slate covered with figures in front of the camera before the scene was photographed this strip of film now bears its own index figure to aid the factory later in assembling the complete picture.

Next, the scene showing the return of the thief over the fence, his scuffle with the watchman, and his escape is to be taken. This will probably require many more rehearsals than the previous scene, both that the action be properly vigorous and realistic, and that the players be drilled so that they will not inadvertently cross the camera lines in the heat of the action. An audience would naturally not take very kindly to a scene in which a man was fighting with an adversary who could not be seen, which would be the case should one of the players step outside the lines while the other remained in view of the camera. It is even possible that many strips of film will be wasted before the scene is taken in a manner to satisfy the director.

Now we pass within the grounds. There is a brief scene to be taken as the thief starts to climb the wall on making his escape, and also the short one showing him running across the lawn to the house. He is to make his entry by way of a window, and the camera is placed so as to view the one chosen. The same procedure is followed here—numbering of the scene, rehearsals, including a preliminary timing of the action so that the director will know how many feet of film it will take, and then photographing, after which preparations are made for the next scene. The director and his players may easily put in a busy day about the house. There will be scenes showing detectives, summoned by the householder, examining the grounds, the watchman hastening up to the front door after he has recovered from the blow inflicted by the thief, and so on. When the sun finally gets too low for the camera's liking it will be a tired but contented party that returns to the studio.

This is but one side of the story. Much has also happened within the house. Though recently perfected portable lighting systems have made it possible to take motion pictures within actual houses, the method is only occasionally used, and our director will probably decide to take all his interiors in the studio. On his return from the day of work outdoors he will leave his requisitions with the carpenter and property-man and be prepared to start early the next morning with his scenes set and all other things ready. Then the thief's entry into the window, as seen from inside the house, his theft of the jewels, we will say, his departure, the householders aroused from their sleep by the watchman, and their consternation at the discovery of the theft will all be photographed. Pieced together and shown on the screen, the various strips of film will tell a smoothly developed story, but we have seen how it is really made up of little bits of action, photographed at different times, and in far from consecutive order. We have seen what a world of planning the director must do before he sets out to make even the simplest scene of his story.

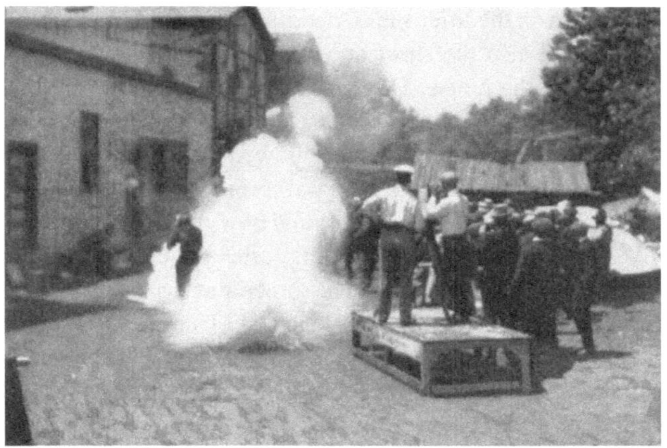

(*Vitagraph*)

Staging a Spectacular Battle Scene

But we have been watching the director while he is working on dramatic scenes that employ only a few players, of whose ability he is certain. Perhaps he has a ball-room scene to take with his interiors, and then there is a busy time indeed ahead of him. He must drill and toil with fifty or a hundred "extras" drafted from the outside and receiving only a few dollars for the day's work. Or else one of his exteriors may call for a player to jump from a bridge. The leading woman will not perform this feat; she is too careful of her own life. So a "double" must be employed—a daredevil of about the same build as the leading woman, and to be dressed in the same clothes. The leading woman will perform the scene until about the point where she leans over the railing preparatory to the fatal leap. Then the camera will be moved to a distant point, and, too far away for the deception to be noted, the "double" will make the thrilling jump. If there is to be a rescue the leading lady will now get herself wet, as we are given close views showing her being pulled from the water, apparently near death from her feat. For such "stunts" as even a daredevil cannot be employed to perform, the property-room may make dummies, "rags and bones and hanks of hair," weighted with sand. Then there are the more spectacular scenes that may test a director's skill, such as battles, fires, and so on. Here he must fortify himself with numbers of trusted assistants, who, dressed like those in the scene, will be scattered among the "extras" where the voice of the director often cannot reach. Hours, and even days, of rehearsal are sometimes necessary in securing such effects. For the battle scenes in "The Birth of a Nation" the producer surrounded himself with a corps of assistants equal to a commanding general's staff. In addition telephones were strung along to all the trenches so that the producer was in touch with every section of the vast battle-field at all times.

V
THE FACTORY

The average amateur photographer, who has made a practice of developing and printing his own photographs, will find little of interest in a description of the stages through which the film passes in a motion-picture factory. It is essentially the same process that he follows, though, naturally, on a much larger scale and making use of all the mechanical appliances possible. The variations in the chemical formulas used are those which the studious amateur's own judgment would dictate to him were he working under conditions similar to those of the motion-picture photographer.

His day's work completed, the camera-man takes his negative film, which is contained in the take-up box of the camera to protect it from the light, to the factory. The film taken from the camera now faces the following steps: the development, washing, and, finally, fixing, thus producing a "negative" from which the "positive" prints used for exhibition purposes are to be made. The development of the negative takes place, of course, in a "dark room," that is, dark in the photographic sense, the sole illumination being that of lamps providing a pure red light. The negative strips are wound spirally about pins on a rectangular rack, thus making it possible to wet the entire surface of the film simultaneously and equally when the rack is submerged in the developing solution.

Metal and hydroquinine are the chemical agents most active in the developing solution most commonly used, soda sulphite, soda carbonate, potassium, metabisulphite, and water completing the formula. But even for standard work there are varieties of developing-baths, while to handle film taken under out-of-the-ordinary conditions still further changes are made. It is in his ability to meet varying circumstances that the factory executive shows his mettle. Test developments may be made on a few inches of film to indicate the exact process to be followed. The washing of the film, and its submersion in the "fixing"-bath are the next items, also familiar to the ordinary photographer. The "fixing"—that is, submersion in a solution of sodium hyposulphite—renders the negative immune to the light, after which it is once more washed, this time to remove the "hypo" of the fixing-bath. The negative may now be treated with a diluted solution of glycerine, which renders it soft and pliable, for there is much wear in store for this negative.

We have seen previously how each scene taken during the day was numbered to aid the producer in assembling the picture in the proper order. The negative strips are now assembled in a complete strip and viewed by the executives of the company before the first positive print is made. This initial inspection will, like as not, show that some of the scenes must be retaken, either because of poor photography or for some other reason not noticed by the director at the time the original scene was taken. "Retakes" are, naturally, not popular with the men who pay the bills, though they are often due to natural causes beyond the power of the director or camera-man to forestall. As picture producers always take a good deal more film than will be used in the subject shown later in the theaters, this viewing of the negative will also aid in bringing the picture down to the required size and in deciding on the printed inserts needed, though it is also probable that a good deal of cutting, reassembling, titling, and so on, will be done after the first positive print is made.

The negative approved, we are now ready to print the positives. On the negative, as the amateur photographer will know, the light conditions were reversed from the normal.

That is, the portions of the film which we would expect to appear white, such as a snow-covered walk, were black, while the dark portions, a railroad train, for example, appeared white. This is the principle explaining the method of printing positives. The negative is superimposed on the positive film stock and light allowed to stream through. Naturally the image on the negative obstructs light in proportion to its density. Our snow-bank, let us say, being black on the negative, will allow no light to pass through and that portion of the positive stock under it will not be exposed. The near-by train, appearing white on the negative, offers no obstruction to the light, and here the positive is strongly exposed. When the positive is later developed it takes on a deposit of silver in equal proportion to the strength of the exposure, the snow-bank taking little, while a heavy deposit of silver clings to that part of the film showing the railroad train, which received so much exposure to the light. Thus the positive print brings the light conditions back to normal again, the train appears dark, the snow white, and the other objects in the scene shaded in ratio to the amount of light they allowed to penetrate through the negative to the positive stock.

In practice positive printing is done by a machine using for its essential principles the shutter and feeding devices that we have seen in the motion-picture camera. Negative and positive stock are perforated alike, and when superimposed the perforations fall in alignment. The film-feeding device of the printer engages in these perforations just as we saw it do in the camera, only in this case it is moving the negative and positive film along simultaneously. What would be the lens in the camera is here the place where the light is allowed to pass through. Once more the shutter serves its purpose of shutting off the light while the required length of film for one small picture is shifted into place. As in the camera, care is taken that the light strikes no portion of the film but the three-quarter-inch strip that is being exposed. The action of a printer is practically automatic, but the human touch is evident in determining the brilliancy of the light, its distance from the film, and the speed at which the printer will be run, all points determined by the condition of the negative.

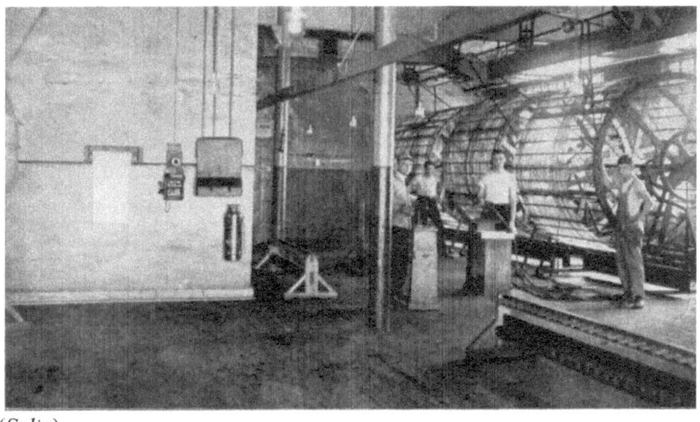

(*Selig*)

Drying-Room in the Factory—The Film is Wound on the Large Drums

The developing of positive film is a process much similar to that we have just described for the negative film. The chemicals used in the formulas are much the same, though the proportions vary. As positive film is less sensitive to light than negative, the developing need not be done in a dark room, though even here daylight, or the "yellow" light of the common electric bulb, is not permissible. To the eye positive and negative film appear much alike, and, in truth, they differ only slightly to render them more adaptable to their different uses. The drying of both positive and negative film, following the various operations, is accomplished by means of large drums, on which hundreds of feet may be wound.

The picture producer may now decide to tint some portions of his film and to tone others. Tinting is nothing more than giving the film a bath of dye; toning is a chemical process by which the dark portions of a picture are intensified and given certain color tones, while the high lights are not affected. Though photography at night is now attempted very frequently, tinting is the means more commonly employed to give the impression of action taking place at night. Toning does not appear so artificial as tinting, since it does not affect the high lights, and an artistic director may easily arrange his scene so that the coloring appears natural on those parts that are affected. The toning of film is accomplished by placing it in chemicals which affect the silver deposits on the surface, permanently changing its color. Where there is no silver deposit, as, for instance, in the snow-bank we have so often mentioned, there would be no change. The process of fixing follows.

It might be well to explain here the usual method of photographing subtitles and other explanatory reading-matter in a picture. This is done by means of an ordinary camera using glass plates, which points downward at the subtitle, which is in white letters on a black background. What is known as a "plate-printer" is then used to put this impression on the positive motion-picture film. In this process the transparent negative of the subtitle secured on the glass plate is placed in a cabinet between a condenser lens and a smaller projecting lens. Before this small lens there is a film-gate, the positive film being fed into it in the same manner that we have seen employed in the camera and the positive-printer for ordinary work. Thus when the light passes through the condenser and the negative of the subtitle, the small lens casts a reduced image of it on the small bit of positive film passing before the gate. In ordinary printing of motion-picture film negative and positive are superimposed and passed before a light; in this case the image cast by the small lens takes the place of the negative film, but the principle is the same.

The factories of motion-picture plants must be as delicately handled as any piece of intricate machinery. The temperatures of the various rooms, and also of the chemical baths used in the different processes, must be kept constant at certain points. Dust must be conspicuous by its absence, for the slightest particle of foreign matter may scratch and otherwise harm valuable film. The water used in the factory is an important item, and in cases where the regular supply has been shown to be inferior by chemical analysis, picture companies have often gone to the expense of drilling artesian wells to secure a pure supply. This was one of the moves made at a factory near Philadelphia, which boasts of its ability to turn out six million feet of positive film each week. Though most motion pictures made in the United States are produced in California, practically all of the factory work is done in the East. This is largely due to the fact that New York is the distributing point and business center. Not all of the companies known for their film productions have developing and printing plants. Many of the factories do the mechanical work for numerous other firms. In addition there are scores of companies doing only factory work and staging no pictures of their own.

The picture is now all but ready for the market. Most of the directors take part in the assembling stage when the film is cut to its proper length, the subtitles inserted, and the finishing touches applied that make the picture ready to meet the eyes of the outside world. This is indeed one of the most important stages in the making of a picture, for here the work of the best of directors may easily be unalterably ruined, or, perhaps, a poorly staged picture made into a passable or even good one.

It is an impossibility for a director in staging a picture to photograph just the amount of film that will be required for the production that is offered to the public. In the first place, even the most experienced of picture-men cannot hope to accurately estimate the amount of film that will be needed to portray certain actions; and secondly, a director will often find, when he has his players working before the camera, that a certain scene is worthy of more space than originally planned for in the script. So that, even after throwing out the scenes that were spoiled for one reason or other, there is still some paring to be done before the picture is cut to the length that the film editor thinks the subject worth and the business office says is most likely to be profitable. Commercial reasons still demand, for instance, that pictures consist of a certain number of full reels, each containing approximately one thousand feet. If the film editor finds that his picture is at its best at five thousand three hundred feet he faces the unwelcome task of cutting three hundred more feet, though each scene now in the picture may appear to him essential. Natural-length pictures, which would run the exact length demanded by the story, with the remainder of the reel, if necessary, filled out with an appropriate short picture, are frequently seen, and their advocates are many. But they are not in strong favor commercially.

VI
THE BUSINESS SIDE

The business organization of the motion-picture field can find no counterpart in any other line of commercial activity. In some of its aspects it is akin to the theatrical world, in others it resembles publishing, but there are many points distinctly unique. The commercial organization is an evolution peculiarly adapted to picture conditions, and it is still in a state of transition, continuous and even more radical than that evident in the producing methods.

In its most interesting feature the system used in the United States resembles the newspaper syndicate, through which an article is published simultaneously all over the country in dozens of newspapers. In this case the article is supplied to the different newspapers in advance, with the statement that it is "released" on a certain date; that is, the newspaper may publish it on and after that particular date, but not before. This explains the surprise of the young man who travels away from home for the first time when he finds that the newspapers of the city he is visiting carry many of the special features he reads in the papers at his home city, and that they publish the articles simultaneously. In a similar manner motion pictures are shipped far in advance to the exchanges, the local distributing agents. A certain "release" date has been chosen, and on that day the picture is shown for the first time in theaters throughout the country. New York, in the heart of the film world, thus boasts of no advantage over the city a thousand miles away. The use of the word "release" in this connection is similar to that in the newspaper syndicate field, which explains a point that invariably proves confusing to the layman seeking information in filmland.

We are told in the chapter dealing with the history of the motion picture of the formation of the first large distributing organization. The system followed by this combination will give an idea of the method employed by the older organizations in handling the short pictures that make up the bulk of the film output. In forming the combination a group of pioneer picture manufacturers bound themselves together to release their product to the theater-owners through the one channel. Exchanges are located in the principal cities of the country and the distributing organization purchases from the manufacturer the number of positive prints of each picture needed to supply these exchanges. A manufacturer's popularity with the exhibitors and the public is shown, of course, by the number of positive prints that the distributor must purchase from him to meet the demand. These manufacturers profited both by the sale of their prints and, through their direct interest in the distributor, from the earnings of the latter. There are two other large distributing agents organized along the lines of the pioneer to handle the output of other manufacturers. In the one the union between producer and distributor is not as close as that of the pioneer, while in the other producer and distributor are practically identical.

From these distributing agents the theater-owner secures his program, the usual practice being to pay a stated weekly rental price, dependent on the number of reels he secures and their freshness. The exhibitor who shows the pictures on the day they are released naturally pays a proportionately larger rental for this "first-run" privilege than the theater-owner who is satisfied with pictures that may be days or weeks old. The latter runs the risk of showing pictures that his patrons have already seen in other theaters, and, naturally, he must expect film that has received the wear and tear of many performances since the day it was released.

This method sufficed for the short picture, but the

coming of the feature, a production of three or more reels, changed matters considerably. It brought a score of independent producers into the field, and these men set about seeking their own methods of marketing. The first step was the development of "state rights" buyers, usually independent exchange owners who bid for the exclusive rights to handle the feature productions in their territories. The producer sold the rights and the necessary positive prints for the different territories to the highest bidders, and after that he washed his hands of the production, though, of course, he still had the negative, should additional positive prints be needed. The purchaser of the "state rights" was now in absolute control of the picture in his territory. His income was secured by renting the picture to the theater-owners.

"State rights" are at present heard of only seldom; they have been succeeded by the "feature program," a combination of manufacturers of long pictures similar in many ways to the older combinations of the producers of short pictures. The chief advantage of the feature program lies in its certainty. To the theater-owner it offers an assurance of a steady supply of pictures of a certain quality, and in addition he knows the pictures that he will show far enough in advance to properly advertise them. To the picture producer the feature program offers a steady market, with an income that he can estimate, and thus he is enabled to make greater expenditures on each picture and to plan more extensively for the future than would be the case were each production to be sold separately.

Each of the feature programs has its own type of organization. Some are practically closed corporations handling only the productions of a certain group of manufacturers. Others are comparatively elastic in their organization, and, while releasing all the productions of certain manufacturers, will also contract to handle the pictures made by independent workers. The manufacturer usually receives his income from the feature program through a percentage of the rental earnings of his pictures. In the case of distributors who sign monthly or yearly contracts with exhibitors to supply them with a stated number of pictures each week it can be seen that the manufacturer's return will be almost a constant figure, affected only slightly by the merits of the individual picture. This is, in fact, one of the most important defects of the closely bound program, it tends to place all the pictures on a common level. While this may work to the producer's advantage in the case of a poor picture, he also finds it irksome when he attempts to secure the proper return from a picture that cost him an unusually large amount to produce. The feature program that secures its income from the per diem rentals of each picture, with no long-term contracts to fall back upon, is a trifle more elastic.

We now come to the latest step in the evolution of the business side of the motion picture. This is, in many ways, a return to the methods of the theatrical producer. The manufacturers found that they could not expect to secure a reasonable profit from pictures that cost extra-large sums of money and many months of preparation if they were marketed through the ordinary channels. So they resolved to take a leaf from the stage producer's book and turn exhibitors themselves. With such productions as "The Birth of a Nation" the manufacturer handles the presentation himself in the large cities, and the picture, like the spoken play, is presented as long as it attracts patrons. If the picture succeeds, an engagement to packed houses of many weeks, or even months, is assured, so that it can be seen that the manufacturer's profits are tremendous. Different methods are used following the metropolitan engagements. Sometimes the manufacturer will sell the rights to the territory he has not touched, just as in the old days he sold "state rights." Or perhaps he will send out many different prints of the picture to tour the country under his own management in the same manner that the theatrical manager sends out a number of companies to present the piece that has succeeded in New York. The original company will be seen only in New York, and possibly Chicago and a few other large cities, while the other companies will tour the "one-night stands," up and down the map. Just as the prestige of success in New York aids a play, so it also proves valuable to a picture.

The earnings of a motion-picture production are as fluctuating as the rise and fall of stock prices in Wall Street. The cost of a thousand-foot picture is usually placed at the average of a thousand dollars, and the manufacturer selling his positive prints at ten cents a foot and releasing through established channels markets twenty-five prints, though the number may run many more or less, according to the efficiency of the selling organization and the popularity of the particular type of picture. He may thus be seen to have more than doubled his investment. His foreign sales may double this figure again. But this instance treats of the manufacturer who has been years in business, and who is releasing through one of the combinations strong enough to practically guarantee a market. Even in these cases inferior-quality pictures or a change in the tastes of the public may quickly force a drop in the number of prints sold. Likewise it does not require a very great increase in the cost of production to eat up the profit.

The manufacturer of long pictures faces even greater uncertainty. His investment in each picture will average between ten and twenty-five thousand dollars, and it does not require many high-salaried stars or spectacular scenes to reach the higher figure. Nor have we considered the overhead expense of maintaining a studio and offices and the heavy outlay to market the picture. A poor picture can lose all of the original investment and even more, the latter if a strenuous effort is made by means of advertising and so on to sell it. A good picture can double the investment, and the outlook for a picture of unusual strength is rosy indeed. Many very costly productions have been forgotten a month after they were released; many very good pictures are still earning money for their producers two and three years after they first came on the market. The life of the negative is without limit, and after the original investment has been recovered, the cost of supplying new positive prints for those that have worn out is a small item.

Theater-owners who show the long-feature productions pay an average of fifty dollars per day for the rental. If competition is strong between the producers the price may go lower, and long-term contracts to use the output of certain organizations may also make the cost of his pictures less to the theater-owner. But frequently he will pay more than this sum for the picture that has proven its popularity. The theater using short pictures—showing three or more subjects at a performance—contracts for its service at a stated weekly rental price, ranging from fifty dollars to two hundred and fifty dollars or more. For the top-notch price he will receive "first-run" pictures, that is, pictures he is allowed to show on the day of release. For the intermediate price his program will be varied; it is apt to include one "first-run" picture, one week-old subject, and others that have been released a greater length of time.

VII
PRACTICAL HINTS ON PHOTOPLAY-WRITING

In a preceding chapter we have endeavored to drive home what we conceive to be the first and most important lesson in the art of photoplay-writing; that is, a respect for the work and willingness to devote serious attention and study it. Regardless of what the correspondence-school advertisements say, writing photoplays is no easy task, and selling them a still more difficult one. The screen is not a retreat for hackneyed, broken-down plots that failed of a sale everywhere else, nor is it likely to pay you for the idea that you dash off in a few idle moments. True enough, you can see many mediocre stories, many trashy ones, when you attend the picture theater, but the aspirant for success should not take the worst specimens for his ideal. It is bad enough for the staff writer to be forced to turn out such material to keep step with the swift pace of production, but the fact that he can do it so much easier than the outsider means that the latter's efforts must be top-notch to bring forth the welcome check that comes with acceptance.

The would-be photoplaywright must first undergo a process of self-examination. He must be certain that he possesses the power of observation that enables him to see the germs of stories in the little incidents that would ordinarily be passed by with scarce a moment's thought. He must be gifted with the imagination that will enable him to create a full-bodied story—a plot—from this germ. Lastly, he must possess the story-telling ability, or, more properly for photoplay-writing, the knowledge of dramatic principles necessary to relate his story in such a manner that the interest of his audience mounts steadily and is held to the end. These qualities the beginner must have at the outset. He can learn later the possibilities and limitations of the silent drama by studying the pictures in the theaters. Likewise, by imitation of a sample form he can learn how to prepare his manuscript in the correct technical form.

Let us take up in greater detail the necessary qualities that we have enumerated. We will imagine that you have pencil and paper before you and have set out to write a photoplay. Your brain is barren of ideas, but you can't afford to wait for an inspiration; you might sit there all day, chewing the end of your pencil, before a plot-germ would come to you out of the empty air. But there is your note-book—first aid to the power of observation—let's see if there is anything there to jog the imagination. Turning the pages of the note-book, you see brief jottings that represent weeks of observation. Here is a note prompted by a newspaper account of a train hold up in which the lone bandit blunderingly made away with the mail-bag, leaving thousands of dollars in currency untouched. The newspapers said the laugh was on the robber, but as you read the thought flashed through your mind, "Supposing a fugitive from justice, wrongfully accused, knew that in the mail carried by this train there was a letter concerning the condition of his wife who was critically ill back East, and that he braved arrest and possible death, not for money, but because of the strength of his love?"

There are possibilities in that idea, but somehow or other, as you revolve it in your mind now, your enthusiasm does not increase. For one thing, you know that newspaper accounts are dangerous bits of inspiration. Possibly fifty or a hundred other photoplay writers in all parts of the country have read the same story, followed similar lines of thought, and are about to write stories with this as the central idea. The staff writers have also seized upon it. Then, again, the only plots your imagination gives you to build around the idea are trite and ordinary. So you decide to let this plot-germ rest in the note-book until some future moment, when another jotting, or perhaps a bit of happy inspiration, will give you the material to make a strong, original story out of it.

Over the pages of the note-book you go again. There are accounts of humorous little incidents that you witnessed or heard about, and which will one day furnish inspiration for comedies. There are notes concerning unusual faces, features that, to an observant eye, seem to be pregnant with stories. A two-line note may describe the odd-looking house you saw on your walk last Sunday that brought to mind visions of ghosts and goblins. This is what we mean by the power of observation. Without it you cannot hope to succeed as an author, for there is no such thing as inspiration *per se*; observation is the seed of inspiration. Cultivate this power, use your note-book, never lose a moment in search of an idea, spend your time developing the plot-germs that you have found at the best of sources—real life.

"The ability to create a plot from this idea," we have stated as the second important quality. "Plot"—there is the stumbling-block that halts the majority of beginners. "The biggest defect of the plays submitted by outsiders," says Lawrence McCloskey, a photoplay editor who has handled thousands of such manuscripts, "is that they do not contain real plots. They are usually abstract incidents, more or less interesting, but without complications sufficient to hold the attention of an audience. Or else they are in the nature of long histories, telling the life stories of their characters, without definite beginning, climax, or ending."

What is plot? In Editor McCloskey's sentence you have the outlines of a definition. It is not an abstract incident, or even a series of such incidents. It is a story woven around a central theme, which is usually a crisis in the lives of the characters. It has a definite beginning, which is at the time when the causes are born which gradually increase in strength and at the last give rise to the events which produce the climax, the height of the suspense and interest. It has a definite ending, which should come as soon as it has been determined whether the crisis overwhelms the characters or whether they pass through it successfully. The ideal plot is the plot of struggle, whether physical or mental. The struggle may be that of two men for the favor of a girl, a poor man against starvation, an avaricious one for wealth, or it may be the struggle of a woman to keep steadfast her faith in a worthless husband. The climax is the point at which the struggle becomes most bitter, the outcome of which is to decide whether the characters win or lose in their fight against odds. The climax may be in sight to the audience soon after the beginning; in fact, a grouping of the early incidents so that the audience fears the climax produces suspense, but the outcome, the author's solution of his climax, must be in doubt. Or, if it be sensed by the audience, the means by which he is to bring it about must be the author's secret until he is ready to say the word. There are students who go further in the analysis of the subdivisions of a plot, and in dividing the different types, but the beginner who uses this definition as a test of his stories will not go wrong.

We will go back to the note-book and seek an idea that may be developed into a plot. Here is a hastily made note written to remind you of a pathetic face: "The wrinkled old woman and the worried-looking daughter who come to the post-office every day." "Aha," you say. "Here is a ready-made plot. I'll have them coming to the post-office in search of a letter from a wandering son. They are in poverty, and just as they are about to be turned out of their home I'll have the son return laden with wealth." Beware of the ready-made plot! The studio mails are full of them, but no checks are drawn to pay the authors. The judge who condemns his own son, the little child who reforms the burglar, the upright district attorney who defies his sweetheart's father, the political boss, all these are old friends of the photoplay editors. "But," you say, "I saw one of these same stories on the screen only a few days ago." Perhaps you did, but think it over. Wasn't there something else besides this bare idea, wasn't there some new twist, some original turn that lent it freshness and almost made you forget how old the plot-basis was? Let's see if we can't take the idea about the old woman and daughter at the post-office and give it a new guise. And before we start to mold our plot remember that we can't compel the characters to do what we want them to do; we must give them a reason for every action. In real life people do not do things without a motive or an impelling cause, but many photoplay authors would seem to think that the fact that the author wanted his characters to perform a certain action is sufficient excuse for it. To check up: Originality and consistency are all-important. Seek a fresh viewpoint, but when you get something new remember that it must be logical, let it not insult the intelligence of the audience.

Starting out, then, we need a reason for the son going away from home. Suppose we change the young woman's status and make her, not the daughter, but the girl who was to have married the son. They quarreled, she broke the engagement, and in a state of mingled temper and despair he ran away. Soon after his departure the mother is injured in an accident and her sight destroyed. Blaming her pride for the son's leaving home, the young woman takes upon her shoulders the care of the mother. The son takes to drink and roistering companions; he descends lower and lower in the scale until finally he is a besotted tramp. We now have our characters drawn; we have a reason for the son's action in leaving home, an "excuse" for his long absence and apparent indifference to what is happening there, and a motive for the girl in seeking to make the mother happy.

All well enough. We have our characters, but we are still far from having a story. An audience might be mildly interested in such people, but there would be no gripping suspense, no desire to know more concerning them. There would be no "doubt as to outcome" because from all appearances the lives of the characters are to continue in the same channel. We want "complications," but don't go after them like the average beginner and throw in action and befuddling incidents just for the sake of mixing things up until you are ready to have the son return home. And don't fall back on the trite story we have already discarded—the mother in poverty and the son returning in time to save her. Let's see: Mother and sweetheart are hoping for the son's return, the audience expects to see him back. Can't we introduce some element that would make his return also a cause for fear? Steer clear of that thought that tells you, "He went away charged with a crime, and he will brave arrest to come back to his dying mother's bedside." The audience knows that story too well. We have it! When the mother met with the accident the doctors despaired of her life. To make her last few weeks of life more happy the girl concocted imaginary letters from the son saying that he was prospering in a distant country. Later, when death seemed near, to cheer the mother and strengthen her faith in her boy the girl's letters told of his efforts to return home, though the means of travel were difficult. But finicky fate ruled that the mother, though still blind, should recover her health, and the girl has been forced to continue the deception. Now the surgeon holds out hope that within a few months the mother's eyesight may be restored. Here we have complications and suspense galore. Any way out seems to lead to trouble worse than any which our characters have yet encountered.

We are nearing the climax, and you will find that long ago the plot has taken the reins into its own hands; it needs no more spurring. Through the rooms of the darkened house there one day sounds the mother's cry, "I see! I see!" After the first glad embrace of the girl her cry is for her son's letters. Desperate, the girl urges her to wait until the morrow, after the surgeon has said that she may read. While the mother is protesting the girl suddenly tears herself away and flees hysterically from the house. She walks blindly down the hillside to the railroad tracks, then throws herself down on the grass to weep. She hears voices. Peering through a near-by bush, she sees a gathering of tramps hovering over a fire, a whisky-bottle passing around the circle. Frightened, she turns to run, but a slight noise betrays her, and the tramps, drink-crazed, start after her. All but one run only a few steps, but this one, more daring than the rest, continues the pursuit. She stumbles and he comes upon her. With a despairing scream she turns to look into his leering face, and—it is the son and sweetheart.

There is your climax. End your story in any one of the many ways that are possible, but, above all, end it quickly. It is a wise author who knows when his story is done. Withstand the temptation to start another story at the point where this one ends. You do not have to follow your characters to the grave; the interest of the audience is over when the crisis is past. You may spoil the effect of a good story by trifling with its interest after that. That is part of the story-teller's art that we spoke of as the third essential—the ability to know where to begin the story, so that no time is lost in useless detail, while at the same time making the necessary points clear, a knowledge of what incidents to introduce and how to group them so that they merge smoothly into the climax and the gift of stopping when the story is done.

Thus far our talk has been on points that might apply with almost equal force to any line of literary endeavor. Let us now take up some points more closely identified with the photoplay. We have learned how to look for ideas, we have seen how a plot is built; now we must find out how to tell our story on the screen. It should be unnecessary to tell aspirants that since all photoplays are told by means of pantomime, "action" is a prime necessity. The audience wants to see the characters do everything worth while in the story. It feels cheated if you insert a subtitle saying, "Helen loves John because he saved her from death in a factory fire." The screen's purpose is to show the fire, to show John performing his heroic deed. No matter how good your story is, if it is of such a type that it cannot be "acted out," then it does not belong on the screen. Printed inserts are unwelcome necessities—they are not the substance of which the motion picture's popularity is made. Cultivate the "picture eye," the faculty of visualizing each incident in your story, to discover if it is possible of being explained to an audience by means of action without the aid of words.

Make each scene tell its own story, either by carrying the action of the whole a step further, or by giving an insight into the character of a person important in the story. For instance, instead of the bald statement, "John Jenks is a crusty old bachelor," why not a scene showing Jenks in his home irascibly ordering his servants about?—let the audience see for itself the type of man he is. Have your scenes follow one another logically, but—here the printed insert shows its usefulness—don't show uninteresting action that can be covered by a brief subtitle. For example, if your characters are at the seashore for one scene, and the next important bit of action occurs at the city home, instead of the uninteresting scenes showing the characters boarding a train, arriving in the city and so on, use a brief insert, "Back in the City," and take up your action there. The insert saves a lot of uninteresting action that would only bore the audience, while on the other hand, if you were to switch your characters suddenly from the seashore to the city without a word of explanation the spectator would be mystified and in doubt as to just what was happening.

Remember that the more principal characters you introduce in your story the more difficult you make it for the audience to follow the thread of the plot. Of course, you can have all the minor characters, such as servants, that you like, but have your story told by the actions of a few principals. This regard for simplicity should be followed in the manner of telling your story.

"What subjects are in demand?" For the outside writer the market is always best for the shorter pictures, comedies or dramas running one, two, or three reels in length. Comedies of merit are in greatest demand, not because more comedies are produced—the reverse is actually the case—but because less good comedy is written. Follow the pictures that are being shown in the theaters if you would keep in definite touch with the studio demands, or else read one of the trade journals that give theater-owners advance information of the pictures that are to be produced.

The trade journals will also be your guide when it comes to selling your photoplay. By reading the manufacturers' advertisements there you will learn the type of picture each company is producing, and this is the first and most important lesson in the marketing of photoplays. Follow the players, and if you have a story especially suited to a certain player send it to his company first. The trade papers must also supply you with your list of addresses, for any roster printed in a book is certain to be out of date within a few months after the book is off the press.

Typewrite your manuscript. Here are other rules of the game which the beginner often disregards: Write on only one side of the paper; use white paper about eight and a half by eleven; put your name and address on the first page of the manuscript; and, most important of all, inclose a stamped and addressed envelope for the return of the story should it be unavailable. Make carbon copies of all your stories.

Make certain that your story is good by all the tests you can devise, and then pin your faith to it and keep it in the mails until it sells. Don't hesitate to rewrite it, however, if after a few months you feel that it can be improved.

Were we asked to confine our advice to would-be photoplaywrights to one sentence, we could give no better hint than, "Study the screen." There, in three words, is contained the one big secret of success in the picture field. See all the pictures you can, occasionally see them more than once, and *study* them.

VIII
TECHNIQUE OF THE PHOTOPLAY

For the purpose of making clear the strictly technical aspects of photoplay-writing it has been decided best to provide a model "scenario," as the manuscript form of the photoplay is called. Explanatory notations are made on the different points in construction developed. From the model given here the beginner will understand the manner in which he must develop his story, scene by scene, telling of each move made by the characters.

"How many scenes are there in one reel?" is a question often asked by beginners, when a little thought should show them that the number will vary, depending on the length of the individual scenes. The average is between thirty-five and forty. It will be seen that the model runs over forty, but many of the scenes are the briefest of flashes. Remember, "a scene is the action that can be photographed without stopping the camera." No matter how short your scene seems, if you feel that the camera-man would have to stop grinding, and move his camera to take in the next action, then you know that the next action must be numbered as another scene. The form for photoplays of more than one reel is similar to that given here. The author may suit his own convenience in deciding whether to number his scenes from beginning to end of the story or to number each reel separately.

The author is indebted to the Edison Company for the privilege of using the scenario of the one-reel photoplay, "Across the Great Divide," by Edward C. Taylor. The notes in brackets are solely explanatory and are not part of the scenario.

If you desire, an outer sheet may carry the name of the photoplay, the number of reels, whether it is comedy or drama, your name and address, and a line, "Submitted at usual rates." The first page proper of your scenario will read:

(In upper corner author's name and address)

"ACROSS THE GREAT DIVIDE"

SYNOPSIS

Bob Carson, a young man from the country, leaves for the city in order that he may earn enough money to marry Mary Carter. After several years of plodding effort he is shown as a telegraph operator in a Rocky Mountain station. Black Jack and his band plan to hold up a train carrying a large shipment of gold, and, in order that their crime may be covered up, decide to cause a head-on collision. They force Carson to send the message that will cause the accident, under the cover of their guns, with the certainty that if he refuses he will be killed and Black Jack, an ex-telegrapher, will send the message himself. Immediately afterward he receives a message apprising him that his sweetheart is dead. With nothing left in life to live for he jumps to the telegraph instrument and, before the bandit realizes what he is doing, countermands his orders, saying as he does so: "There will be no wreck now. We will meet across the Great Divide." As the last click of the instrument ceases, the bandit, realizing what he has done, shoots him dead.

[From three hundred to five hundred words should suffice for your synopsis. Have it tell all the important points of your story, but don't go into unnecessary detail that the action scenario can explain. The synopsis is the most important part of your manuscript; it is the first thing the editor reads—and often the last. Make it clear, convincing, and brief—your sale depends largely on it.]

The second page:

CAST OF CHARACTERS

Bob Carson—Young country lad, later a telegrapher.
Mary Carter—His sweetheart, country dress, sunbonnet, etc.
Black Jack—Heavy-set desperado.
Bird Stevens—Outlaw, lieutenant of Black Jack.
Red—Shifty-eyed, suspicious-looking character.
Another telegrapher.
Superintendent.
Call-boy.
Four other desperados.
Boy to represent Carson at age of twelve.
Carson's mother.

[Some of these players will appear for but a few seconds, but you must list every character to appear on the screen. Brief descriptions will suffice unless you want some particular type.]

SCENES

Interior:

Attic room—5.
Rocky Mountain despatch-office—8, 11, 16, 20, 29, 31, 32, 33, 34, 36, 37, 38, 39, 41, 43, 44, 45, 46.
Section of day-coach—10.
Section-house, sleeping-bunks, 40.

Exterior:

Farm-yard—1, 3, 9.
River-wharf—2, 4, 6.
Western Union city office—6.
Cut through rocky gorge—12, 14.
Woods near railroad track—13.
Clearing in woods—15.
Mountain road—17.
Small station—18, 28, 30, 42.
Clearing on ridge—22.

Railroad tracks near station—23.
Another section of mountain road—19.
Cross-roads—24.
Tree with swing—21.
Woods, with despatch-office in sight—25.
Bushes at side of railroad track—26.
Down railroad track as seen from 26—27, 35.

[The figures denote the number of the scenes in which the different locations are used. List every location or setting used in this scene plot. Be sparing in your use of interior scenes where exteriors will serve the purpose equally well. Interiors increase the cost of a production in time and expenditure for scenes.]

Start a new page:

"ACROSS THE GREAT DIVIDE"

Scene 1. *New England farm-yard.*
> Carson with old-fashioned portmanteau on scene. Calls Mary, she appears, they embrace. He bids her good-by, telling her he is going West to make a home for her. She breaks down as he exits.

Scene 2. *On a Chicago River wharf.*
Subtitle: Six weeks later. In Chicago destitute.
> Carson dejected, clothes baggy, gazing into river. Dissolve into—

Scene 3. *Farm-yard, same as 1.*
> Mary stands alone. Wistful expression. Dissolve back to—

Scene 4. *Wharf, same as 2.*
> Carson still on wharf. Express despair. Brightens. Dissolve to—

Scene 5. *Attic room.*

Carson, twelve years old, studying telegraphy, picking at instrument, following instructions in book. Mother enters and scolds, making him study school-books. Dissolve back to—

Scene 6. *Wharf; as in 2.*

Carson goes off to follow up inspiration.

[The subtitle is here inserted before Scene 2 to prepare the audience for the break in the action. While it says that Carson is destitute, the action of the scene carries the explanation still further. Don't let your subtitle spoil the scene by telling too much. By dissolving the other scenes, that is, narrowing the lens so that they "fade" in and out, the audience knows that they represent Carson's thoughts. An abrupt change of scene would mystify the audience. In practice the director may decide to use double exposure for these scenes, but it is best for the author to leave these special effects to the producer's discretion.]

Scene 7.

Exterior Western Union city office.

Carson comes out of office with long tickets in hand. Pauses to register, "Thank God!" and happiness. Exits.

[To "register" means to convey a certain feeling to the audience. The long tickets let the spectator know that Carson is going a great distance, without the necessity of an abrupt subtitle stating the fact.]

Scene 8.

Interior Rocky Mountain despatch-office.

Subtitle: Six years have passed.

Other telegrapher at instrument receiving message. Carson enters, with dinner-pail, to relieve him. Greetings, etc., other telegrapher exits. Carson reserved and thoughtful. Lights pipe, and settles in chair. Fade to—

Scene 9. *Farm-yard, same as 1.*
Carson bidding Mary farewell.
[The author desires to show us that, though he is far away in the wilderness, Carson's thoughts are still true to Mary.]

Scene 10.
Close-up of seat in moving day-coach.
Red finishes writing note. Handwriting to be irregular owing to train motion.
Flash—note: *Big haul on No. 5, first car. Fargo shipment. $300,000 yellowbacks, no guard except messenger. (Signed) Red.*
After tying note on spear-handle, conceals same, and exits.

Scene 11. *Despatch-office, as in 8.*
Close-up of Carson receiving message.
Flash—message on official blank: *No. 5 carrying pay-car East—*
[These "flashes," unlike subtitles, are not to be printed statements, but are reproductions of the particular object, a newspaper clipping, letter, telegram, etc., and are inserted in the body of scenes as indicated. Make them brief; long letters mean many feet of film to give the audience time to read them.]

Scene 12.
Rocky gorge. Railroad tracks.
Rear of day-coach pulling out of scene. Informer Red on platform, slings spiked stick into telegraph post from steps of car.

Scene 13. *Woods near Scene 12.*
Branches of bush part. Black Jack peers through. Plows through bushes.

Scene 14. *Railroad tracks, as in 12.*
Receding train in distance. Black Jack comes on, yanks spike from post.

Scene 15. *Clearing in woods.*
Desperados lounging about. Black Jack enters, unrolls note, reads, and gives orders.
Subtitle: "Stick No. 5 up at Mason's Cut. We'll cover up the job by making the despatcher drive No. 2 into No. 5."
At his last word four desperados exit left. Black Jack and Bird Stevens go off right.

[Note the strength gained by inserting the subtitle in the action of the scene and having it a speech by one of the characters. How much weaker would it have been had the author put his subtitle before or after the scene, and said, "The desperados decide to hold up No. 5 at Mason's Cut and cover up their crime by forcing the despatcher to drive No. 2 into No. 5."]

Scene 16. *Despatch-office, as in 8.*
Call-boy sitting in reckless position, reading novel. Carson orders him to put up signal lamps—no ears. Carson tosses heavy object on floor near him and boy nearly falls out of chair; starts off on "hot-foot" with lanterns.

[The audience must now be kept in touch with events happening at different points. The flashes of the desperados will show them moving toward a definite object, and we are satisfied. If we were shown the despatch-office, however, with Carson seated idly at his key, the scene would appear unnecessary, so the author introduces such "business" as that of the call-boy above. The author must hold his audience's interest while bringing his characters together for the climax. However, don't let such "business" be important enough to distract the attention from the main plot.]

Scene 17. *Mountain road.*

Black Jack and Bird cantering.

Scene 18. *Exterior of station.*
Call-boy reading novel and lighting lantern without taking eyes off book. Match burning fingers. Finishes job hastily.

Scene 19.
Another section of mountain road.
Black Jack and Bird turn off main road into wood road.

Scene 20. *Despatch-office, as in 8.*
Carson in reflective attitude. Dissolve, or a double exposure of—

Scene 21. *Big knotty tree, with swing.*
Carson swinging Mary. Look much younger.

Scene 22.
Clearing on ridge; station can be seen below.
Black Jack and Bird walk to brink of hill, point down, both start to descend.

Scene 23. *Railroad tracks.*
Call-boy walking with switch signal lights, nose in novel, stubs bare toe, sprawls up holding toe, down track limping.

Scene 24. *Forked roads.*
Four desperados cantering, pass sign-post: "Mason's Cut, 1 mile."

Scene 25.
Woods opposite despatch-office.
Black Jack and Bird take observations; way is clear; start across.

Scene 26.

At Mason's Cut—railroad tracks.

Four bandits arrive, conceal themselves at points of vantage.

Scene 27.

Down railroad track from 26.

Train No. 5 in distance, rounding curve.

Scene 28.

Exterior of station, as in 18.

Black Jack sees poster near door with his picture. Reads: "$1000 reward for the capture, either dead or alive, of Jack Rindge, generally known as Black Jack. Was railroad despatch operator 1898 to 1907. Description:" (Follow with description of Black Jack.) Latter does bravado business, posts Bird as guard, and enters station.

[Two purposes are served by the author's introduction of this poster. He has let us know that Black Jack is an unusually desperate character from the fact that so large a reward is offered, and, of even greater importance to the story, he has told us that Black Jack is a capable telegraph operator. Both are points necessary to the plot later on and skill is shown in introducing them indirectly now. How unconvincing it would have been to have Black Jack say later to Carson, "I am an old telegrapher operator," and thus give the audience its first intimation of the fact.]

Scene 29. *Despatch-office, as in 8.*

Carson studying train report. Office door being cautiously opened. Black Jack steps stealthily into room, covering Carson with automatic, closes door. Carson quickly turns. Carson registers, "Black Jack." Latter makes threatening move toward Carson's hands, saying, "Stick 'em up." Carson hesitates, then slowly raises hands. Outlaw steps quickly behind and searches him, takes position in front of Carson.

Scene 30.

Exterior of station, as in 18.

Close-up of Bird seated on door-step with Winchester across knee. Leisurely rolls cigarette.

Scene 31.

Interior despatch-office, as in 8.

Black Jack studying order-book, tosses it on table, steps back on sleeping cat's tail, disconcerted for a moment. Turns to kick cat. Carson about to leap at him. Black Jack turns back quickly, shoves automatic under Carson's nose and backs him into seat. Keeping Carson covered, Black Jack settles down at table, studying order-book. Speaks—

Subtitle: "Stick out a red for No. 2 at Wind River."

Carson sends message.

Scene 32.

Close-up of desk.

Black Jack searches around until he finds railroad-map.

Scene 33.

Close-up of special railroad-map.

Black Jack tracing plans on map. (To be cut into Scenes 33 and 34.)

Scene 34. *Despatch-office, as in 8.*

Black Jack giving another order: "Give No. 5 order to meet No. 2 at Big Bend instead of Napavin." Carson turns quickly on Black Jack in defiant manner. Registers, "For God's sake, man, do you know that means a human slaughter?" Black Jack laughs mercilessly. Carson, strongly protesting, finally refuses. Black Jack leaps closer. "Send it, or I'll bore you through and send it myself." Carson realizes Black Jack is master of situation any way he decides. Slowly he comes to a decision, finally he reaches forward to key. Expression of Black Jack's face shows what he is sending. Black Jack nods approval.

Scene 35.
Down railroad track, as in 27.
    Train No. 5 coming nearer.

Scene 36. *Despatch-office, as in 8.*
    Black Jack becoming sociable. Carson silent, as if under spell.

Scene 37.
Close-up of Western Union sounder working.

Scene 38. *Despatch-office, as in 8.*
Carson's interest centers on Western Union receiver, ignoring Black Jack's presence. Writes—
Flash—close view of pad as he writes:
From Bradford, N. H.

Bob Carson, Castle Rock, Colo.
Mary's dying wish was to have you know that all her love and last words were for you, and that she hoped to meet you across the great divide.—Mrs. A. L. Carter.
    Remorse creeps over Carson; shows weakness and thoughtfulness; gradually takes on strength and purpose. Offers a little prayer; his hand shoots forward to key. Black Jack up on his feet.

Scene 39.
Close-up of two men over desk.
    Black Jack registers, "Get away from that key." Carson, working like mad, every muscle tense. Carson registers, "There'll be no wreck to-night." Sending message.
Flash—message: *Hold No—*
Black Jack steps back, fires. Carson grasps breast, rises,

slumps back into chair, falls forward on table. Black Jack studies him.

Scene 40.
Interior of section-house, with bunks.
Superintendent and other telegrapher hear shot, pile out of bunks.

Scene 41. *Despatch-office, as in 8.*
Black Jack, walking over to Carson, places revolver in hand, saying, "Remember, you committed suicide." Bravado business; turns away, laughing. Carson weakly rolls over. Looks at revolver in hand in dazed manner; sees Black Jack, takes feeble aim, fires. Black Jack lunges forward, dead.

Scene 42.
Exterior of station, as in 18.
Telegrapher and superintendent rushing up track, partly dressed. Bird fires. Fire returned, Bird topples over.

Scene 43. *Despatch-office, as in 8.*
Carson, apparently dead, moves as if awakening from deep slumber, feebly arises to half-sitting and half-lying position. Wearing a queer little tired smile, feebly gropes as if in dark for the key, sends message.
Subtitle: "Put 5 into clear for 2—quick."
Door bursts open, superintendent and telegrapher rush in. All suddenly tense.

Scene 44.
Close-up view of sounder working, as in 37.

Scene 45. *Despatch-office, as in 8.*
Superintendent takes pad, begins to write.
Flash—close-up view of pad as he writes: *O. S. No. 2 by 3. 42. No. 5 heading out. Attempted hold up in express-*

car discovered, bandits captured.

Scene 46. *Despatch-office, as in 8.*

Carson smiles wearily. Registers: "Black Jack got me. He was going to put them together to cover up the robbery. I gave all I had, boys. That's all; I'm going now. She is waiting for me over there." Slight flutter, scene fades.

IX
PICTURE-PRODUCING BY AMATEURS

Motion pictures have become so intimate a part of our life that it is only natural to see amateur theatrical societies and other organizations becoming interested to the point of staging their own productions.

To the amateur the ideal manner of staging a motion picture is, of course, to handle every detail of the production within the organization, merely going outside to rent a camera, purchase film stock, and finally for the factory work of developing and printing the film. The pleasure of "doing everything yourself" is almost too great to be resisted, but if a successful production is to be assured it is wise to call on professional help in other branches. Unless the organization has within its ranks a photographer of more than ordinary ability, who is willing to spend some time and money in preliminary study of the motion-picture camera, and in wasting film in experimentation, it is necessary that a professional camera-man be engaged. Again, were the organization to decide to dispense with the services of a professional photographer it might be necessary to purchase a camera—at prices ranging from two hundred and fifty dollars upward—since it would probably be difficult to find a company willing to intrust one of its cameras on rental to an amateur.

Should the organization be willing to go a step further in seeking the aid of professionals, the services of a capable motion-picture director would go a long way toward the betterment of the final production. We believe it possible for an amateur with the dramatic sense, following the director's method of work as outlined in this book, to stage a satisfactory picture without the services of a professional director. But this would depend largely on the quality of the co-operation extended by the camera-man.

Let us proceed in this chapter on the assumption that you have decided to engage a professional camera-man, but you are going to place your trust for all other details on your own members.

The cost—that is the first question the amateur asks, and, naturally, the one that must be settled before any organization will embark on such a venture as the staging of a motion picture. We have told you in a preceding chapter that the film-producing companies calculate the cost of the average picture at one dollar per foot. With the amateur organization conditions are of course different, and this estimate furnishes no basis of comparison. In enumerating the items of expense to the amateur we must first consider the cost of film stock. This is about three and three-quarters cents per foot; positive film is a trifle higher than negative, but this figure may be taken as an average. It must be understood that there is always more film stock used than the length of the finished production would indicate. We will say that you intend to produce a three-reel picture, running approximately three thousand feet and providing three-quarters of an hour of entertainment. About four thousand feet of film would be used—a moderate estimate—allowing one thousand feet for film spoiled or omitted from the picture in the final assembling to improve the continuity and clarity of the story. The raw stock for the negative and positive prints would therefore cost three hundred dollars.

Then there would be the expense of developing the negative and printing the positive, which, including the printed inserts, would be about six cents per foot. The cost of our three-reel film, with one thousand feet allowed for waste, would now be two hundred and forty dollars, plus the cost of the raw stock, or five hundred and forty dollars. These calculations are based on the average market prices, though slight variations must of course be expected.

With the matter of film and printing settled, we take up expenses that cannot be so definitely decided. Under ordinary conditions the staging of a three-reel picture by amateurs should require about four weeks, somewhat longer than the professional would take, but not as long as the amateurs will require, unless the members are determined to work hard and use every available moment of sunshine until the picture is completed. Our estimate of four weeks is based on the understanding that the amateurs will be ready to start work at nine o'clock in the morning and, with the exception of a little over an hour for lunch, work until five o'clock. The salary of a photographer, supplying his own camera, would be between one hundred and one hundred and fifty dollars per week. The cost of our production now jumps from five hundred and forty dollars to ten hundred and forty dollars, figuring the camera-man's salary at one hundred and twenty-five dollars per week. If it should be decided to engage a director the organization will be able to find capable men at salaries starting at the two-hundred-dollar level.

The salaries of players and the expense of purchasing a story do not enter into our calculations here. The matter of costuming is one that should not trouble the amateur either, for his story should be written so as to make the lightest of demands in this regard. The members of the organization should also be able to secure the necessary permission for the use of all exterior settings without paying for the privilege, as the film-manufacturing concerns must often do. It is also possible for the author of the story to so construct it that no interior settings are necessary, thus obviating the expense of engaging a studio or else of paying for portable lights to be used in the actual interiors mentioned in the story. The advantages offered by the locality in which the story is to be pictured will determine the decision to be made on these points. There is another point to consider; only organizations located near film-producing centers will be able to rent studios without the expense of transportation for the company.

On the story depends in great measure the success or failure of an amateur effort at screen production. While the principal idea, the plot, may be the work of one man, the work of production should not begin until every point in it has been threshed out by the combined wisdom of all the members of the committee in charge of the production. Test each bit of the action to see that it can be done with your facilities; don't attempt an elaborate story and then be forced to rewrite it after the work of production has started. That means time lost—for which you are paying salaries—and a weakened production. Construct a story, as has been said above, that uses exterior scenes almost entirely. See that the locations are convenient; it does not require many journeys from one end of the town to the other to eat up valuable time. Don't hesitate to use the same setting more than once. The points enumerated here would appear to be only "common sense," yet it is our experience with the efforts of amateur photoplaywrights that they invariably lift the check-reins from their imaginations, allow the story to wander up hill and down dale, and seem to make a special effort to have each bit of action take place in an entirely new location.

If the organization holds within its membership-lists some players of more than ordinary ability it might be possible to successfully stage an ambitious drama. For productions of this type the light comedy form is, however, best suited. The rôles, being more natural, are better handled by the players, while at the showing of the picture the audience, instead of being in the seriously critical frame of mind induced by a drama, is receptive and ready to overlook minor faults. The exaggerated melodrama is probably the greatest favorite with amateurs.

Remember the words of advice in a preceding chapter about limiting the number of principal characters, and avoid the danger of confusing the audience by having too many important rôles. This is a matter for delicate handling in amateur productions where many members will be found to feel that they should not be slighted. It is of value in increasing the interest to include in the picture at least one or two scenes in which all the members of the organization have an opportunity to be photographed. A lawn fête, political meeting, or any such affair may be the justification for their appearing in the picture. But see that some action of value in the unfolding of your story happens in this scene, for it must appear natural, and not as if it were dragged in by the collar.

Give to the man you name "director" supreme charge after the story has been approved by the committee and the work of production is about to start. Except perhaps for evening conferences to decide on the next day's plan of work the time has now arrived to place entire command in the hands of one man. Let him decide the order in which the scenes are to be taken, issue the "calls" for the players needed each day, rehearse the scenes, and give the final word when he deems it time to photograph the scene. The director should not be a person who is to play a part in the picture, unless it is to appear in one of the scenes we have mentioned which will allow the entire membership to be seen.

The director should have two assistants, a "location" man and a "property" man. The "location-man's" task is to seek the various spots that will be used as settings and to make the necessary arrangements with the owners for their use on the date set. The "property-man" must see that all the necessary paraphernalia, such as carriages, swords, letters, or any article needed in the different scenes, is on hand and ready for use when the director calls. Both these aides must work from two to three days in advance of the director, so that there will be no annoying delays because a certain spot cannot be used on the day desired, or because a table and chair needed in one of the scenes is not at hand. These assistants, or others appointed, should also watch the staging of the scenes, with especial care for the minor details that might escape the eye of the director who is sufficiently burdened in seeking to interpret the story. The assistants, for example, will make notes of the clothes worn by the players in the different scenes, so that, a week later, when scenes are being taken that in the story are supposed to happen on the same day, there will be no absurd mistakes. Unless careful notes are made of these matters it is easy to slip and show us, when the picture is exhibited, a character starting out on an auto ride with a soft hat, Norfolk coat, and soft-collared shirt, only to arrive at his destination wearing a golfing-cap, severely cut business jacket, and immaculate in a stiff linen collar. In the case of female characters, with their more extensive wardrobes and innate desire for change, this danger of ridiculous errors is magnified. The lot of the director's assistants will not be an easy one.

For the director himself the methods of work have been outlined in a preceding chapter. First, in collaboration with his assistants, a "scene plot" is laid out; that is, a list of the locations needed, and the number of the scenes in which they will be used. Similarly a "property" list is made out. Let him also determine, as we have shown the professional director doing, the order in which he will stage his scenes. A convenient plan now is to have the complete scenario typewritten, each scene on a separate sheet of paper, and placed in a loose-leaf binding in the order decided upon for production. The director will find that this makes it much easier to study the individual scenes thoroughly, to so "visualize" them as to secure their full possibilities.

In taking the scenes, let the director remember one particular point: Rehearse, rehearse, rehearse, before the camera is turned an inch. Once the camera starts to "grind" you are using film, and if everything is not perfect you are either wasting money on scenes that will have to be retaken, or else you are weakening the picture should the faults be overlooked. In rehearsing, the director must not only assure himself that the players are capably interpreting the emotions called for by the story, but he must also see that there is no danger of their stepping outside the lines of the camera's vision in the excitement of the action after photography has started. Experience with two or three scenes will show the director that this happens more often than would seem possible. Before the final word of approval is given the players must go through their parts as though they were "second nature," for the camera registers everything, and the look to the side-lines, the glance at the director for instructions that would go by unnoticed on the stage, will be caught by the camera and cannot be erased except by taking the scene over again.

After a rehearsal or two the camera-man will time the scene for the director so that he can tell how much film it will use, and if it is not in agreement with the estimate allowed in the scenario, make the necessary changes. The camera-man will lay out the boundary-lines of the stage for you and advise you on the distance from the camera to station the players. This will vary according to the number of characters in the scene and size of the stage required for the particular bit of action. For ordinary scenes it is wise not to allow the players to be farther than fifteen feet from the camera, and frequently for a tense bit of action in which a few players are seen they should be brought up to the ten-foot line. In acting the players should move a trifle slower, more deliberately, than they ordinarily would.

The length of your scenes is limited by the film capacity of the camera, usually two hundred feet. This would mean a scene of about three minutes' duration, but you should be sparing in your use of scenes even approaching this length, as it does not require many of them to eat up an entire picture. If it should be necessary in developing the story to use a very long scene, see if some means of variation cannot be introduced by showing some bit of action in the story transpiring at some other point. Three minutes seem very short to the layman, but if you will time some of the scenes in the next picture you see you will find that very few run even a fourth that length.

If you do not happen to be near one of the large film-producing centers where there are plenty of laboratories, your camera-man may be relied on for advice in locating a plant to develop and print the film. It will be wise for the director to make the journey to the film plant and view the picture and assemble it there.

For showing to the organization's members and friends a local theater may be secured; or else, should it be decided to use the clubhouse, a projection-machine can be rented and an operator engaged. Reference to the telephone-book of the nearest large city will give you the names of many accessory companies providing machines and operators for such engagements. It will probably be necessary, to comply with the local fire-department rules, to rent a portable asbestos booth. Rules vary, but you are apt to save considerable eleventh-hour trouble if you get in touch with the local fire and building departments before attempting to show the picture.

A parting word as to the time of the year to stage your picture. This will vary in some parts of the country of course, but in general it may be said that the spring and summer are the ideal times. Not only are conditions for exterior work not pleasant in the fall and winter, but a light snow-fall which you would imagine would only delay the picture a day may easily hold it up for many more until all the snow is off the ground, for otherwise you face the danger of showing scenes supposed to happen on the same day with snow on the ground in one view and none in sight in another.

THE END